London's Cemeteries

by Darren Beach

D0814444

London's Cemeteries

Written by Darren Beach
Photography by Susi Koch & Andrew Kershman
Edited by Abigail Willis
Illustrations by Lesley Gilmour & Hannah Kershman
Design by Susi Koch and Lesley Gilmour

3rd edition published in 2019 by
Metro Publications Ltd
metropublications.com

Metro® is a registered trade mark of Associated
Newspapers Limited. The METRO mark is under licence
from Associated Newspapers Limited.

Printed and bound in China. This book is produced using
paper from registered sustainable and managed sources.
Suppliers have provided both LEI and MUTU certification.

© Metro Publication 2019
British Library Cataloguing in Publication Data.
A catalogue record for this book is available from the
British Library.

ISBN   978-1-902910-63-5

To my wonderful wife, my amazing son,
and my Mum and Dad. I love you all.

Acknowledgements

I would like to thank the staff of all the cemeteries I visited, phoned and contacted for information. Their help and insights were invaluable. I am also indebted to the many 'Friends' organisations who helped with my research. These voluntary groups do a fantastic job of helping to maintain and renovate London's cemeteries, and have contributed a great deal in making them such wonderful places to visit. My thanks also to Andrew Kershman at Metro Publications for giving me the chance to write this book. A special thanks too to the late Sue Bailey, whose http://londoncemeteries.co.uk blog was an inspiration, for her help, encouragement and wonderful photography. Finally I want to thank my wife Tomo for putting up with me spending weekends away trawling London's cemeteries, and the endless evenings when I sat typing away in silence at my laptop!

Central London Cemeteries

for full list see page 12

GOLDERS GREEN
CREMATORIUM

+ HOOP LANE
JEWISH CEMETERY

ARCHWAY RD

HAMPSTEAD
HEATH

HIGHGATE
CEMETERY

HAMPSTEAD
CEMETERY

SHOOT UP HILL

FINCHLEY ROAD

HAVERSTOCK HILL

CAMDEN

ST P
OLD

ALPERTON
CEMETERY

WILLESDEN NEW
CEMETERY

HARROW ROAD

ST MARY'S
CATHOLIC CEMETERY

PADDINGTON OLD
CEMETERY

MAIDA VALE

REGENT'S
PARK

ACTON
CEMETERY

WESTERN AVE

KENSAL GREEN
CEMETERY

MARYLEBONE ROAD

HANGER LANE

WESTWAY

OXFORD STREET

THE VALE

BAYSWATER ROAD

KENSINGTON
PARK

HYDE PARK
PET CEMETERY

HYDE PARK

PICCADILLY

SOUTH EALING
CEMETERY

GUNNERSBURY
CEMETERY

KING ST

WESTMINSTER
ABBEY

MARGRAVINE
CEMETERY

BROMPTON
CEMETERY

KING'S ROAD

CHELSEA EMBANKMENT

MORTLAKE
CREMATORIUM
& HAMMERSMITH
NEW CEMETERY

CHISWICK NEW
CEMETERY

GREAT WEST ROAD

BARNES COMMON
CEMETERY

FULHAM ROAD

BATTERSEA
PARK

BATTERSEA PARK ROAD

WANDSW

CHISWICK OLD
CEMETERY

PUTNEY LOWER
COMMON CEMETERY

NORTH SHEEN
CEMETERY

OLD MORTLAKE
CEMETERY

UPPER RICHMOND ROAD

River Thames

ST MARY MAGDALEN'S
MORTLAKE

ST MARY'S CEMETERY
BATTERSEA

CLAPHAM
COMMON

EAST SHEEN
CEMETERY

PUTNEY HILL

HUGUENOT
BURIAL GROUND

RICHMOND
CEMETERY

RICHMOND
PARK

TRINITY ROAD

WANDSWORTH
CEMETERY

ROEHAMPTON VALE

MERTON RD

LAMBETH CEMETERY
& CREMATORIUM

PUTNEY VALE
CEMETERY

GAP ROAD
CEMETERY

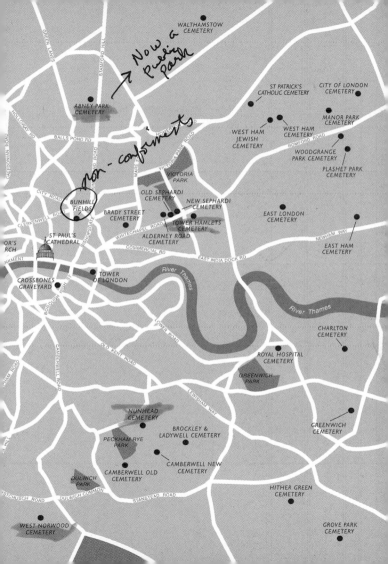

Contents

"All human life is laid
bare in a cemetery."
Norman Lebrecht, 2004

Introduction

Why write a book about London's cemeteries?

During my research for the first edition of the book a number of people expressed surprise that anyone should be interested in what to them seemed a series of identikit gardens full of stones. The response to the book has proved that I am not alone in my fascination for the magnificent cemeteries, those temples to eternity, dotted around London.

There are still those who do not understand that cemeteries offer us an accurate reflection of London's social, economic and ethnic history, as well as being a treasury of fascinating stories, courtesy of their permanent residents. For those uninterested in history, cemeteries can always be treated as alternative parks where frisbees and boisterous behaviour are banned in favour of gentle strolling.

Of course many people already make use of London's cemeteries without the encouragement of this book. In the course of my research I have witnessed people jogging, strolling, eating, reading, talking, playing hide-and-seek, sleeping and even having sex (or at least hunting for a potential partner). Some cemeteries, such as Highgate, have recognised the public interest and provide guided tours and maps, while others feature permanent educational and wildlife centres.

Writing this book has been a considerable task – there are 124 municipal cemeteries within London's boundaries, as well as several more in private hands, including uniquely Jewish, Muslim and Roman Catholic cemeteries. The cemeteries which feature in the following pages are the ones I consider to be the most interesting, historic and worthy of visiting in and around Greater London. I have also managed to find a few more favourites for this new edition of the book.

My aim in writing this guide has been to provide an informative, occasionally off-beat, look at London's cemeteries and to show how visiting them can be an enjoyable and memorable experience.

What makes us so fascinated by cemeteries?

Cemeteries enable us to step into the past. They are places of peace and tranquillity but in them we get a sense of London's social history – of the struggles and divisions between rich and poor. Cemeteries are full of unique personal histories – just look along the rows of headstones to find tales of infant mortality, of war, of the hardships of the industrial age.

Death is the great leveller. Ordinary folk who lived their lives amiably and without spectacular achievement can lie for eternity alongside statesmen, scientists, musicians, actors, pioneers, the famous and the infamous. In London's cemeteries you will see mausoleums next to simple plain graves. The graves of the anonymous are often fascinating, but in death as in life it is the famous who attract the greatest curiosity.

The architecture, inscriptions and symbols of London's cemeteries are eloquent of the ritual surrounding the ultimate taboo of death. There is a great deal of grand sculpture to admire in the cemeteries of London in what heritage expert Hugh Meller has called 'a galaxy of Victorian funerary art'. This type of art delighted in symbolism and a glossary has been provided at the end of this book to help readers make sense of the snakes, doves, eagles and obelisks they are likely to encounter (see page 275).

How did cemeteries become so important?

The foundations of London's grand cemeteries were laid in the Victorian age of reform and progress, when many ad hoc medieval institutions were overthrown and new arrangements established in their stead. A more detailed account of how the major cemeteries came into being after 1830 to accommodate over crowding can be found in the chapter entitled 'The Magnificent Seven Cemeteries' (see page 6). It is worth noting here that these cemeteries are a product and reflection of that great epoch in British history.

Initially cemeteries were built by private enterprise but the newer, suburban cemeteries that subsequently sprang up in London's outer limits were under municipal control. Britain was in the grip of a revolution as the newly emergent middle class assumed centre stage in Victorian society, even shaping the behaviour of the monarchy itself. This numerous, socially mobile and confident class were determined to leave their mark on history and one way they planned to do this was by grand monuments, solemn ceremonials and lavish funerals.

How did cemeteries develop in the 20th century?
In the 20th century the business of burial came full circle, as the problem of overcrowding returned. By the end of the Second World War, around 50% of London's cemeteries were either full or approaching capacity. The arrival of the Green Belt, to help protect London's surrounding open land, immediately increased the pressure on whatever open spaces remained. At the same time post-war demands for new housing, roads and services for the living pushed up the value of land.

It also became far too expensive to be buried locally. Today it can cost more than £1,000 per burial for residents of the borough the cemetery is located in – for non-residents, who may have a long family connection with the area, it can be much more. Not surprisingly, many Londoners these days are being laid to rest far from the city where they lived their lives.

The problems of the 20th century were in part alleviated by a significant court ruling in 1884 concerning a Dr Price, who was charged with illegally burning his son's body. The judge decreed that there was no law against cremation providing it was done without causing ocular or nasal offence. This was taken as the go ahead by the Cremation Society and the first legal cremation in England took place in 1885 at Woking. The majority of Londoners are now cremated – in London the cremation rate went up from 4% in 1945 to over 70% in 1985. This trend was helped by a change in the Catholic Church's attitude to cremation in the 1960s.

All London borough councils have a burials authority, but none is under any obligation to provide or maintain cemeteries. A lot of cemeteries have fallen into dereliction, but some of the larger ones receive the support of charitable societies to help restore and renovate them. All the magnificent seven cemeteries benefit from dedicated, public spirited 'friends' organisations which have helped transform wastelands into places really worth visiting.

What about the future?

Statistics issued by the Museum of London in October 2000 showed that Inner London boroughs had on average seven years' burial space left. In fact, just four years later both Tower Hamlets and Hackney boroughs announced that all their cemeteries were full, and more parts of London are sure to follow. At that time academics and professionals agreed that it was necessary to start reusing existing graves, something that had once been deemed unthinkable.

This consensus helped shape the debate when it came to the passing of the Local Authorities Act (2007) which encourages the reusing of old graves. In order to ease the shortage of burial land a system of 'lift and deepen' has been adopted, under which existing remains could be re-interred at a much deeper level, leaving room for three or four 'new fill' coffins above them. Tim Morris, chief executive of the Institute of Cemetery and Crematorium Management, has spoken in favour of reusing graves, saying: 'It's a desperate situation. We need to think about the bereaved, but also those yet to be bereaved.' In other words, reuse is probably the only way cemeteries can survive into the future.

The increase in cremations in the post-war period has helped the situation but there is still a growing problem of space. Julie Rugg of York University's Cemetery Research Group has been quoted as saying (The Guardian, November 2000): 'Even where people are being cremated, more are choosing to bury the remains with a memorial. People are finding they want somewhere to go back to.'

The snappily-named 2008 Dead Citizens' Charter stressed the need to urgently reduce overcrowding in cemeteries. If not enough is done then London runs the risk of its 'entire legacy of splendid cemeteries deteriorating into unkempt, derelict, dangerous, useless blots on the landscape' according to Giles Dolphin in a 2002 GLA report.

The issue is riddled with ethical dilemmas but a decision will have to be reached. All concerned are agreed that cemeteries must be places where the dead are allowed to lie undisturbed with dignity and respect; but equally, cemeteries have to be renovated, maintained and care taken to ensure they don't fall into neglect. Poor maintenance and vandalism have been a major problem in recent years and with a shortage of housing for the living it is not surprising that cemetery funding is low on local authorities' list of priorities. The Greater London Authority does appear to be aware of the problem and some action is being taken. In 2005 the Forest Park Cemetery and Crematorium in Ilford became the largest multi-faith cemetery to be opened in London for 40 years.

What can I, the visitor, do at cemeteries?

Well, firstly, just enjoy the escape from urban London. Wander among the famous names of Highgate or Putney Vale, take a stroll along the wide, verdant avenue of the City of London Cemetery and take time to appreciate that you are walking through London's past. Some cemeteries, such as Nunhead, offer spectacular views of the city and their grounds are home to the kind of wildlife and plants you don't see in the course of a normal urban day. Pause for thought at incredible architecture, some of which could grace a museum but instead lies covered in moss and leaves. Above all, take the opportunity to reflect how London, and the world, have changed since London's first cemetery opened at Kensal Green in 1833.

The Magnificent Seven Cemeteries

& the rise and fall of the first garden cemeteries

Kensal Green Cemetery

Imagine if London's population in 2050 was over 20 million. How would everyone fit into the city? But there has been a precedent for dealing with such a vast increase – it happened almost two hundred years ago.

The first half of the 19th century saw the population of London rise from 1 million to 2.3 million. One of the results of such rapid population growth was a serious lack of burial space, with churches brimming with burials. Instances grew of body snatching, of bodies left out to rot or not being buried deep enough, of bodies cleared from graves too soon, and the kind of sanitary problems not seen in London since the Plague, as cholera began to spread rapidly.

By 1820 most churchyards in the city were so overcrowded that they were a severe health risk to anyone unlucky enough to be working or living nearby. Thousands of bodies were buried in shallow pits beneath the floorboards of chapels and schools. Church-goers and pupils were forced to endure the putrid stench of death as they went about their daily business.

Something clearly had to be done – and fast. The Chief Officer of the Poor Law Commission, Edwin Chadwick, himself buried in Old Mortlake Cemetery, published a damning report of churchyard overcrowding in the city which recommended wide-ranging reform. As a result Parliament was forced to take notice.

The Victorians looked to private enterprise to solve their burial problem. Enter the concept of 'Garden Cemeteries' as private entrepreneurs solved the burial crisis by creating suburban cemeteries, independent of the parish church, with vast, beautifully landscaped gardens. The idea of using private means to build public cemeteries was nothing new – burial grounds, independent of parish churchyards, had been emerging courtesy of London's Nonconformists throughout the 17th and 18th centuries.

Many of the major influences on the new landscaped public cemeteries came from abroad. The meandering, tomb-lined avenues of Père Lachaise in Paris were much imitated. Before long these new 'garden cemeteries' became popular places in which the moderately well-off Victorian could take a leisurely stroll, at a time when the kind of parks and major urban spaces for which London is renowned did not yet truly exist.

The Government decided to capitalize on the entrepreneurs' ideas. In July 1832, Parliament passed 'The Act for Establishing a General Cemetery for the Interment of the Dead in the Neighbourhood of the Metropolis' which encouraged the establishment of seven public cemeteries in a ring around the periphery of London. The act was passed unanimously, not least because of the cholera epidemic of that year. In fact, it had even been deemed necessary to bring back the plague pit system that hadn't been used since the 1660s. Such a turn of events embarrassed the House of Commons into action.

In 1833 Kensal Green Cemetery was the first to be established on a vast 72 acre site with separate chapels for Anglicans and Dissenters. South London's South Metropolitan Cemetery – now known as West Norwood Cemetery – followed in 1837 and north London's Highgate in 1839. Nunhead, Brompton and Abney Park arrived a year later, and Tower Hamlets in 1841. These 'new' cemeteries are what we now know as the Magnificent Seven, and were created with the stated intention of finally solving the problem of the terribly overcrowded graveyards throughout the city.

Until this point, private cemeteries functioned alongside these new public cemeteries, but legislation was passed in the 1850s which forced urban churchyards to close. From that moment on, municipal cemeteries became the dominant force. They had an instant appeal to the emerging middle classes, who were keen to show how far they had risen and demonstrate that in death, as in life, they had some real social status. Cemeteries provided a place for families to establish permanent monuments to themselves. The latter part of the 19th century saw the peak of the garden cemetery craze, with the grand spectacle of mourning an essential part of having 'made it' in Victorian society.

London's Cemeteries

A number of factors contributed to the gradual decline of the Magnificent Seven cemeteries as the Victorian era came to a close. One was that the cost of grandiose monuments, memorials, and funerals was proving too much of a burden for most normal people. Another was that cremation was starting to enter the arena as an option – Golders Green Crematorium was an instant hit in 1902. But the main reason was probably a change in attitudes following the death of Queen Victoria in 1901, with a decline in formality in English society. Things were shaken up further by the First World War's vast casualties. Suddenly, with thousands of young men piled into communal or unnamed graves in foreign places, it hardly seemed appropriate to go on aggrandising death with overblown monuments to ordinary folk.

Cemeteries continued to bury people, but those people were spending less on their exits. Consequently, money for maintenance was less forthcoming and the elaborate landscaping of the garden cemeteries began to suffer. Some cemeteries ended up almost as overcrowded and under-managed as the churchyards they had been built to replace. Many became badly neglected and developed into a bizarre form of urban forestry as they passed in and out of public, private and eventually council ownership. Several began to resemble overgrown gardens, with trees, ivy and shrubs allowed to run riot among the rows of headstones.

Nowadays, all the Magnificent Seven have 'Friends' organizations dedicated to their restoration, conservation and maintenance. Some, like Abney Park in Stoke Newington, have been transformed into public parks with the aid of armies of volunteers and a supportive local borough council. Others, like Highgate's untamed west cemetery, have been left to develop into peculiarly wild environments. All these cemeteries are magnificent, opulent examples of Victorian architecture, planning and landscaping. They are an absolute must for any visitor intrigued by the chance to step back in time and get a taste of how Londoners saw themselves over a century ago.

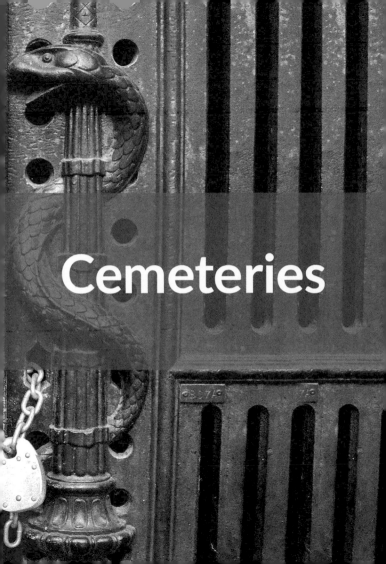

Cemeteries

Cemeteries at a Glance

Bunhill Fields Burial Ground

Central

National Burial Sites

The Actors' Church (1633)

Bedford Street, Covent Garden, WC2E 9ED
Tel: 020 7836 5221
www.actorschurch.org
Transport: Covent Garden LU, Charing Cross Rail; Bus 24, 29, 176
  (Charing Cross Road); Bus 6, 9, 13, 77A, RV1 (Aldwych)
Open: Mon-Fri 8.30am-5pm, Sat depends on events, Sun 9am-10pm

On the west side of Covent Garden Piazza, in Inigo Place, stands St Paul's, The Actors' Church. It was designed by Inigo Jones in the 1630s for the 4th Earl of Bedford, and has enough theatrical connections to make it a must for anyone fascinated by the ghosts of London's theatreland. Nowadays, the church is regularly in demand for events ranging from Christian rock concerts to fundraisers based around the acting world.

Jones toured Italy extensively in his youth, and his obsession with Renaissance architecture dominated his designs – it is thanks to this that we have the continental design of Covent Garden's Piazza, and the church itself.

It may have come to be known as the church where actors chose to be commemorated, but as with most pre-Victorian burial grounds, the churchyard was used to cram as many as possible of the city's less celebrated dead – indeed, the vault beneath the church is said to be full of the graves of London paupers.

Most of the 'vacancies' in the churchyard filled up years ago, as befitting a place nearly 400 years old, but over a century's worth of thespians are commemorated by plaques or memorials, even if they themselves were buried elsewhere. Look out for memorials to giants of the British theatrical world such as **Noel Coward** (1899-1973) and Rochdale's songstress **Gracie Fields**, (1898-1979) as well as world-famous stars like genius **Charlie Chaplin** (1889-1977) and horror maestro **Boris Karloff** (1887-1969).

Gone With The Wind star **Vivien Leigh** (1913-67) demanded a Shakespearean quote for some extra gravitas on her memorial: 'Now boast thee, death, in thy possession lies a lass unparallel'd', from *Antony and Cleopatra*.

It is not only actors who can be found buried here in the centre of tourist London. **Thomas Arne** *(1710-88)*, the man responsible for 'Rule Britannia', the imperialistic anthem that became a football chant, can be found here, as well as the painter **Sir Peter Lely** *(1618-80)*. There is also a stone that marks heart-throb highwayman **Claude Duval** *(1643-70)*, the first 'superstar' thief since Robin Hood, with an inscription that states: 'Here lies DuVall, Reder if male thou art, Look to thy purse, If female to thy heart'.

Inigo Jones himself described the church as 'the handsomest barn in Britain', and though not strictly a cemetery, nor (ahem) a 'lost ark', it is certainly a churchyard worth visiting if strolling through the piazza that defines the epicentre of London.

Notable Residents:

Noel Coward *(1899-1973)* – playwright, composer, actor, singer, composer; **Gracie Fields** *(1898-1979)* – actor, singer, comedienne; **Charlie Chaplin** *(1889-1977)* – comic actor, filmmaker, composer; **Boris Karloff** *(1887-1969)* – actor; **Vivien Leigh** *(1913-67)* – actor; **Thomas Arne** *(1710-78)* – composer; **Sir Peter Lely** *(1618-80)* – painter; **Claude Duval** *(1643-70)* – highway man.

Bunhill Fields Burial Ground (1685)

38 City Road, EC1 2BG
Tel: 020 7374 4127
Transport: Old Street LU/Rail; Bus 43, 76, 141, 205, 214, 271
Open: Mon-Fri 8am-4pm, Sat-Sun 9.30am-4pm (Oct-Mar); Mon-
    Fri 8am-7pm or dusk, Sat-Sun 9.30am-7pm (Apr-Sept)

The vast majority of London's cemeteries date from the period that followed the move away from crowded parish churchyards towards larger 'garden cemeteries'. Yet religious minorities had cemeteries that pre-date even those, and unlike the historic Jewish cemeteries of the East End, Bunhill Fields is large and can be visited with ease.

Hidden between ultra-cool Shoreditch and Hoxton and the buzz of the City, stands this former burial ground for Dissenters, Nonconformists and those who just plain disagreed with organized religion of the 17th, 18th and early 19th centuries. It is also the last survivor of London's once numerous small burial grounds that have long since been lost to bombing, housing and developers. It looks fairly spartan in comparison to the garden cemeteries listed elsewhere, but mature trees overlook the grounds and it remains a genuine haven of tranquillity in among the surrounding city skyscrapers and traffic of nearby Old Street.

The name Bunhill comes from 'Bone Hill', suggesting that there may have been burials at the site since Saxon times. It was first recorded as being set aside as a burial ground during the Great Plague of 1665-66, and was formally established in 1685. Never having been consecrated, it became a popular burial ground for Nonconformists, who were banned from being buried in churchyards because they refused to use the Church of England prayer book. Before long, Bunhill Fields became known as 'the cemetery of Puritan England'.

The monuments to three of England's most famous Nonconformists can easily be seen. The tomb of **John Bunyan** *(1628-88)* is on the left of the large square as you walk in. The author of *The Pilgrim's Progress* was imprisoned for writing theological pamphlets, and the experience formed the background to his epic tale. An obelisk dating from 1870 marks **Daniel Defoe** *(1661-1731)* at the other end of the square. Best known for writing *Robinson Crusoe*, Defoe was also a controversial essayist whose work, *The Shortest Way With Dissenters*, got him into no end of trouble with the establishment.

Behind him, to the right, is a stone that commemorates **William Blake** *(1757-1827)* and in August 2018 this was joined by a newly inscribed ledger stone which lies above his actual burial site elsewhere in the cemetery. Blake combined his work as an esteemed artist with poetry that would grace literature courses for centuries to come. Republicans of all ages may also wish to seek out some members here of Oliver Cromwell's family. Cromwell served as Lord Protector during England's brief republic.

Composer and Dissenter **Isaac Watts** *(1674-1748)* lies here too, in a raised white sarcophagus. It was his old house that would later be the site of Abney Park (see p.35), the cemetery that replaced Bunhill Fields as the main Nonconformist burial site. **John Milton** is not buried here, but the writer of *Paradise Lost* lived in Bunhill Row, on the west side of the cemetery, from 1662 until his death in 1674.

By the mid 19th century the burial ground had become almost full, and Stoke Newington's Abney Park Cemetery had started to reduce the need for burial areas for Dissenters. The City of London took over the administration of Bunhill Fields in 1867 and transformed it into the public open space we know it as today, give or take some repair work in 1960 necessitated by some wartime bombing.

If the Victorian cemeteries tell us volumes about how they celebrated and commemorated the dead, Bunhill Fields gives us a rare glimpse of how London's burial places looked before the large suburban cemeteries were even conceived.

Notable Residents:

John Bunyan *(1628-88)* – author and preacher; **Daniel Defoe** *(1660-1731)* – author; **Susanna Wesley** *(1669-1742)* – mother of the founder of Methodism; **Isaac Watts** *(1674-1748)* – hymn composer; **William Blake** *(1757-1827)* – poet.

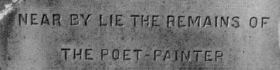

NEAR BY LIE THE REMAINS OF

THE POET-PAINTER

WILLIAM BLAKE

1757 — 1827

AND OF HIS WIFE

CATHERINE SOPHIA

1762 — 1831

National Burial Sites

Long before Edwin Chadwick and his contemporaries of the 1820s came up with the idea of the garden cemetery, the rich, the eminent, the royal and the notorious were being buried in London's three great necropolises – St Paul's Cathedral, Westminster Abbey and the Tower of London. While none of these sightseeing musts are cemeteries as such, their crypts and tombs do contain some of the nation's greatest names.

St Paul's Cathedral (1697)

Ludgate Hill, EC4 8AD
Tel: 020 7246 8350
www.stpauls.co.uk
Transport: St Paul's LU, Blackfriars LU/Rail; Bus 4, 11, 15, 23, 26, 100, 242
Open: Mon-Sat 8.30am-4.15pm
Admission charge: Adults £18, Concessions £16 (Students & 60+)
   Children £8 (16-17), Family £44

The famous and familiar outline of St Paul's Cathedral dominates the London skyline although now surrounded by skyscrapers. It is the fourth cathedral on this site to be dedicated to St Paul, the first dating from 640 AD. After its predecessor was destroyed in the Great Fire of London, Sir Christopher Wren was commissioned to design the cathedral that remains his defining masterpiece.

Of course it is world famous for being the place where royal jubilees have been celebrated, peace services marking the end of the First and Second World Wars have taken place, while in more recent memory the cathedral was the venue for Charles and Diana's ill-fated wedding in 1981.

However, it is in the crypt where we can find the monuments and stone tablets that commemorate those whose funerals took place here. Chief among them are **Arthur Wellesley, Duke of Wellington** *(1769-1851)* and **Horatio Nelson** *(1758-1806),* two men whose heroics during the Napoleonic Wars have made their names, and the decisive battles of Waterloo and Trafalgar, cornerstones of British history. Wellington, who Queen Victoria called 'the greatest man this country has produced', lies in a large brown sarcophagus surrounded by four lions at the foot of a flight of steps, while Nelson's monument is a large sarcophagus placed on a high plinth, set on a floor mosaic that features anchors, sea lions and other maritime imagery.

Wren himself was buried here in 1723, under a raised dark slab in Artists' Corner, where you can also find portrait painter

Sir Joshua Reynolds *(1723-92)* and Royal Academy president **Sir John Everett Millais** *(1829-1896)*. Other names to look out for in the crypt are penicillin pioneer **Sir Alexander Fleming** *(1881-1955)*, *Mikado* and *Pirates of Penzance* composer **Sir Arthur Sullivan** *(1842-1900)* and Labour politician **Sir Stafford Cripps** *(1889-1952)* who served in Churchill's War Cabinet and as Chancellor under Clement Attlee.

After 1936 only ashes were permitted to be buried at St Paul's. There are effigies and fragments of stone that pre-date the present Cathedral, which really are relics of a medieval world. Several monuments exist for eminent folk who are actually buried elsewhere, such as the white marble plaque for Crimean War nurse **Florence Nightingale** *(1820-1910)* and a wall monument commemorating **William Blake** *(1757-1827)*, whose grave can be found a mile or so east in Bunhill Fields.

The only monument to survive the Great Fire in 1666 remains intact, and can be seen just upon entry to the crypt to the right of the pulpit. It is the figure of **John Donne** *(1572-1631)* the poet who later became Dean of St Paul's. You can even see some scorch marks from the fire on its base.

Notable Residents:
Arthur Wellesley, Duke of Wellington *(1769-1851)* – soldier and Prime Minister; **Horatio Nelson** *(1758-1806)* – navy admiral; **Sir Joshua Reynolds** *(1723-92)* – painter, **Sir John Everett Millais** *(1829-1896)* – painter, **Sir Alexander Fleming** *(1881-1955)* – physician, microbiologist and pharmacologist; **Sir Arthur Sullivan** *(1842-1900)* – composer; **Sir Stafford Cripps** *(1889-1952)* – politician; **Florence Nightingale** *(1820-1910)* – nurse; **William Blake** *(1757-1827)* – artist and poet; **John Donne** *(1572-1631)* – poet.

Statue of John Donne

The Tower of London (1066)

The Tower of London, EC3N 4AB
Tel: 0844 482 7777
www.hrp.org.uk
Transport: Tower Hill LU, Tower Gateway (DLR), Fenchurch
    Street & London Bridge Rail; Bus 15, 25, 42, 78, 100, D1
Open: Tues-Sat 9am-5.30pm, Sun-Mon 10am-5.30pm,
    last entry 5pm
Admission charge: Adults £25, Children (5-15) £12,
Concessions £19.50, Family (2 adults, and up to 6 children)
    £45.00
Discounts available for online booking

Founded by William the Conqueror immediately after
vanquishing King Harold at the Battle of Hastings, the Tower was
enlarged and modified by successive monarchs. For centuries the
Tower served as the crown's most important prison holding those
people that were deemed a threat to the State.

The place to go to find the final resting places of those who
were beheaded or hanged either at Tower Hill or within the
Tower's walls is the Chapel Royal of St Peter ad Vincula, right by
the Scaffold Site. The present chapel was erected for King Henry
VIII in 1519-20 – perhaps he knew he'd be utilising it more than
most – but a chapel of some description has probably existed on
the site since before the Norman Conquest. There is no shortage
of superb memorials dotted around its interior and there is also a
wonderful, decorated 17th-century organ.

Three Tudor queens can be found here, two of whom fell
from Henry VIII's favour. To the front of the chapel, there is an
altar marking the resting place of **Anne Boleyn** *(1501-1536)*. She
was the queen whose repeated failure to bear the King a son
brought about her downfall. It probably didn't help, given those
superstitious times, that she had six fingers, odd birthmarks and
a raging temper. **Catherine Howard** *(1521-42)*, Henry's fifth wife,
was an immature young girl who caught the king's roving eye
and whose infidelity led to her downfall. **Lady Jane Grey** *(1537-*

54) was another unwitting victim of Tudor power politics. She succeeded Edward VI in 1554 and reigned for just nine days as a Protestant queen. The following, she was executed, aged just 16, after a plot by her father to overthrow the newly installed Queen Mary was foiled.

The noble blood spilt in the Tower doesn't stop there though. Two legendary Catholic saints lie here, **Sir Thomas More** *(1458-1535)* and **Bishop St. John Fisher** *(1467-1535)*. Both were accused of treason for opposing Henry VIII's decision to secede from the Catholic Church. Fisher declared that 'the King was not, nor could be, by the law of God, Supreme Head of the Church of England', which was the final nail in his coffin. A popular myth has it that after his head was placed on a spike on London Bridge, rather than decomposing as the hot summer days went on, it actually started to look healthier and was hurriedly removed before people started to talk. Both More and Fisher were beatified in 1886 and canonized in 1935.

Invariably, the victims' headless bodies were buried quickly and without ceremony or memorial under the nave. When the chapel was restored in 1876, the remains were unearthed in the nave, and along with some intact coffins, re-interred in the crypt. It is possible to visit the chapel, but visitors need to join a Yeoman Warder's Tour to do so.

Notable Residents:
Anne Boleyn *(1501-36)* – Queen; **Catherine Howard** *(1521-42)* – Queen; **Lady Jane Grey** *(1537-54)* – Queen; **Sir Thomas More** *(1458-1535)* – theologian and statesman; **St. John Fisher** *(1467-1535)* – Bishop.

Sir Isaac Newton

Westminster Abbey (1066)

20 Deans Yard, Parliament Square, SW1P 3PA
Tel: 020 7222 5152
www.westminster-abbey.org
Transport: St James's Park LU, Westminster LU;
    Bus 3, 11, 24, 12, 53, 77A, 88,148, 159, 211,453
Open: Mon-Tue & Thur-Sat 9.30am-4.30pm, Wed 9.30am-7pm, Sun
    closed (Abbey closes one hour after last admission)
Admission charge: Adults £20, Concessions £17, Children (11-18) £9,
    Children (under 11 - accompanied by adult) are free

Westminster Abbey has been the place of the coronation, marriage
and burial of British monarchs since 1066 and is home to the tomb
of the Unknown Soldier, and the shrine of Edward the Confessor
as well as the Coronation Chair, various royal tombs and chapels
and the Abbey's famous Poets' Corner. The current building dates
largely from the 13th to 16th centuries.

Over three thousand people are estimated to be buried in the
church and cloisters of the Abbey. The figure is not exact as proper
records were not kept until 1607, but monuments and medieval
tomb lists help give the number some accuracy. Obviously, not just
anyone gets to be buried at Westminster Abbey – and these days
only ashes are permitted (space being at a premium). Royals take
centre stage, naturally, but eminent Britons from any field can be
considered. **Sir Laurence Olivier** *(1907-1989)*, was interred here in
1991. And then there are employees and servants of the Abbey
itself – Deans, organists, Canons and so on.

The sheer number of eminent folk that can be found here
constitute a who's who of English history. Floor plaques denote the
tombs of poets and writers such as **Geoffrey Chaucer** *(1343-1400)*,
Edmund Spenser *(1552-99)*, **Dr Samuel Johnson** *(1709-84)*, **Charles
Dickens** *(1812-70)*, **Robert Browning** *(1812-89)*, **Lewis Carroll** *(1832-
98)*, **Thomas Hardy** *(1840-1928)* (whose heart is buried in Stinsford,
Dorset according to his family's wishes) and **John Masefield**
(1878-1967), the last poet to be interred here, in 1967. **Ben Jonson**
(1572-1637) is said to have been buried standing up, due to a lack of

available space – his plaque reads *'O Rare Ben Jonson'*. The likes of **Alfred Lord Tennyson** *(1809-1892)* and **Rudyard Kipling** *(1865-1936)* are commemorated by plaques but are buried elsewhere.

Scientists and engineers such as **Sir Isaac Newton** *(1643-1727)* and **Charles Darwin** *(1809-82)*, musicians like **George Frederic Handel** *(1685-1759)* and **Henry Purcell** *(1659-95)*, actors such as **David Garrick** *(1717-79)*, **Sir Henry Irving** *(1838-1905)* and **Dame Sybil Thorndike** *(1882-1976)* have all found a place here.

Britain's political history is represented principally by Prime Ministers **William Pitt the Younger** *(1759-1806)* and **Older** *(1708-78)*, **William Gladstone** *(1809-98)* and post-war Labour Prime Minister **Clement Attlee** *(1883-1967)*.

Other assorted military men, architects and persons of great achievement are scattered around, one of the most prominent of whom is explorer **David Livingstone** *(1813-73)*. I would really like to have a pound for every time someone says *'Dr Livingstone, I presume'* upon seeing his memorial.

Notable Residents:

Sir Laurence Olivier *(1907-89)* – actor; **Geoffrey Chaucer** *(1343-1400)* – author; **Edmund Spenser** *(1552-99)* – poet; **Dr Samuel Johnson** *(1709-84)* – essayist and lexicographer; **Charles Dickens** *(1812-70)* – author; **Robert Browning** *(1812-89)* – poet and playwright; **Lewis Carroll** *(1832-98)* – author; **Thomas Hardy** *(1840-1928)* – author and poet; **John Masefield** *(1878-1967)* – poet; **Ben Jonson** *(1572-1637)* – playwright, poet and actor; **Alfred Lord Tennyson** *(1809-92)* – poet; **Rudyard Kipling** *(1865-1936)* – author; **Sir Isaac Newton** *(1643-1727)*– scientist; **Charles Darwin** *(1809-82)* – scientist; **George Frederic Handel** *(1685-1759)* – composer; **Henry Purcell** *(1659-95)*– composer; **David Garrick** *(1717-79)* – actor; **Sir Henry Irving** *(1838-1905)* – actor; **Dame Sybil Thorndike** *(1882-1976)* – actor; **William Pitt the Younger** *(1759-1806)* – Prime Minister; **William Pitt the Older** *(1708-78)* – Prime Minister; **William Gladstone** *(1809-98)* – Prime Minister; **Clement Attlee** *(1883-1967)* – Prime Minister; **David Livingstone** *(1813-73)* – explorer.

and that He shall stand

at the latter Day

upon the earth

GEORGE FREDER͏IC HANDEL Esqr
born February ⟨...⟩ MDCL XXXIV
died April XIV MDCCLIX.

George Frederic Handel

PARTNER

JIM STANFORD
HORN

THE FINAL CHAPTER

Highgate Cemetery

North

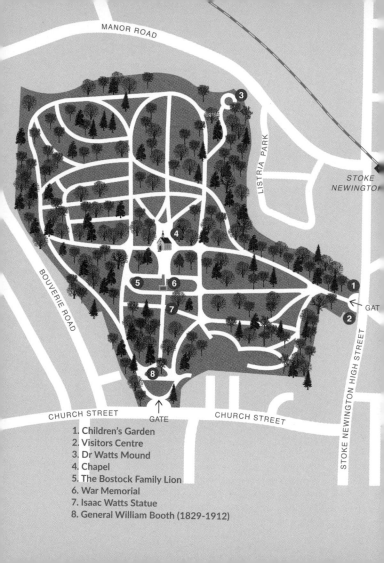

MANOR ROAD

LISTRIA PARK

STOKE NEWINGTO

BOUVERIE ROAD

STOKE NEWINGTON HIGH STREET

GAT

GATE

CHURCH STREET

CHURCH STREET

1. Children's Garden
2. Visitors Centre
3. Dr Watts Mound
4. Chapel
5. The Bostock Family Lion
6. War Memorial
7. Isaac Watts Statue
8. General William Booth (1829-1912)

Abney Park Cemetery (1840)

Abney Park, Stoke Newington High Street, N16 0LH
Tel/Fax: 020 7275 7557
www.abneypark.org
Transport: Stoke Newington Rail (5 min walk);
    Bus 67, 73, 76, 106, 149, 243, 276
Open: Daily 8am-till dusk

The fashionable cafés, boutiques and pretty market stalls of Stoke Newington's Church Street are bordered by a rare jewel in the form of Abney Park Cemetery. Described by Bob Gilbert in *The Great London Way* as 'delightfully overgrown', it manages to be dimly eerie but with the warmth of a cosy municipal park.

The magnificent Egyptian-style ornamental iron gates that welcome you in from the High Street lead into what at first looks more like a park than a cemetery. The unusual hieroglyphs that appear over the loggia read 'The Gates of the Abode of the Mortal Part of Man', and since 1840 those hieroglyphs have symbolised the union between the mortality of man and the beauty of nature at Abney Park.

When it was founded in 1840, Abney Park was unusual in that it was specifically a place for the burial of Nonconformists – those who had rejected the ways of the Church of England, such as Methodists, Baptists and others. It was set up when Bunhill Fields was nearing capacity and, like its predecessor, swiftly became a rallying place for Dissenters.

One of the cemetery's current residents, Sir Thomas Abney, had lived at Abney House in the heart of the Nonconformist district of Stoke Newington, and the house was acquired from well-known Dissenter **Dr Isaac Watts**. Watts joined the Dissenting Academy in Stoke Newington in 1690 and soon became a pastor, writing essays and poems. He is best known for his hugely popular hymns such as *Joy To The World* and *Come We That Love The Lord* which are still performed today and were often written while looking out upon Abney Park from a mound that now bears his name.

In developing Abney Park, the architects chose to integrate the existing grounds of the house with the cemetery plan, by planting over 2,500 varieties of trees and shrubs.

The cemetery's Gothic chapel was part of the original installation of Abney Park. It was designed by William Hosking, who also designed the entrance gates in funereal Egyptian style. Although the spire remains, the chapel, with its original interior panelling, seating and floor removed, is a shadow of its former glory. These days it tends to be in demand as a setting for creepy films, with pigeons swooping around it for added atmosphere.

Something that differentiates Abney Park from other north London 'Magnificent Seven' cemeteries like Highgate and Kensal Green, is the relative absence of overwrought, towering edifices. Not for Stoke Newington the legions of imposing mausolea and extravagant monuments – perhaps a reflection of its Puritan origins. There is still plenty to see here with countless angels, columns, well-proportioned granite and marble monuments, as well as life-size angels, saints and shepherds.

Among the distinguished residents, none are more so than **General William** *(1829-1912)* and his wife **Catherine Booth** *(1829-1890)*, the founders of the Salvation Army, along with their son Branwell who succeeded William as General. Their family plot lies almost directly after the Church Street entrance. The stone that marks the plot is in the shape of a Salvation Army badge, and is backed by wild bushes. Booth was born in 1829, but his stone reads 'Born again of the spirit 1845' to indicate the dawning of his religiosity, when he began to attend Wesley Chapel in Nottingham. Catherine's stone describes her as 'the mother of the Salvation Army'.

A path leads southwards from the chapel and to a series of fine memorials. One of the highlights is a vast, nine feet high statue of the aforementioned **Dr Isaac Watts** *(1674-1748)* (who is actually buried at Bunhill Fields), surrounded by recently refurbished cast-iron railings. An inscription gives an outline of Watts' life.

In Ever Loving Memory of

FRANK C. BOSTOCK.

BORN SEPTEMBER 10TH 1866,
DIED OCTOBER 8TH 1912.

ON THAT HAPPY EASTER MORNING
ALL THE GRAVES THEIR DEAD RESTORE.
FATHER, SISTER, CHILD, AND MOTHER
MEET ONCE MORE.

In Ever Loving Memory of

FRANK TOWER BOSTOCK
DIED JANUARY 1ST 1912
AGED 28 LAST JULY.

FRANCES CONSTANCE MUGLISTON
BORN APRIL 22ND 1893
DIED JUNE 13TH 1954.

FLORENCE EFFIE BOYES
OUR BEST AND DEAREST FRIEND
1875 – 1970.

In Ever Loving Memory of –

FAMILY GRAVE OF FRANK C. AND SUSANNAH
BOSTOCK.

N° 81593

Further along you will pass a marble police helmet under an arch that recalls the heroism of a local policeman, killed while out on duty in Tottenham. There is also a war memorial commemorating local people who fell whilst on active service in two World Wars. You can't miss the central cross with its bronze sword, with bronze plaques naming the dead mounted on the rear wall. This memorial can be found just above the cemetery's catacombs, which are unfortunately now sealed off because of recurrent vandalism.

Close to the War Memorial is one of the most impressive graves to be found at Abney Park depicting a sleeping lion. It marks the resting place of the Bostock family, who were originally Stafford farmers but joined forces with the Wombwell family to form the largest menagerie company in the country. These traveling animal shows were big business at a time when people had no other way of seeing exotic animals. **Frank C. Bostock** *(1866-1912)* was the grandson of the menagerie's founder and became famous for his tours of the United States and introducing the 'big cage' to this country. It is claimed he was the first to use an upturned chair to keep lions under control. His funeral at Abney Park was a major event with over 30 carriages and crowds gathering along the route to pay their last respects. The grave here is identical in style to the Wombwell family grave in Highgate.

A smaller civilian war memorial remembers the many local people who died following enemy air bombardment during the Second World War, in particular 20 people who were killed when flats in nearby Coronation Avenue suffered a direct hit.

A tower-like monument commemorates anti-slavery campaigner **Rev Dr Thomas Binney** *(1798-1874)*, whose cause of death in 1874 was attributed to 'melancholia'. A pristine white block marks the life of **James Braidwood** *(1800-61)*, who is widely regarded as the father of modern firefighting. His death at 61, in the line of duty, led to a funeral procession extending over a mile. Irish Chartist leader **James Bronterre O'Brien** *(1805-1864)* is close by, his tomb marked by a single rose and his portrait. In keeping with the sober aspect of the cemetery's monuments, is the grave of **Mary Hillum** *(1759-1864)*, who according to her gravestone 'died in the same house she was born, scarcely ever slept out of the house in the whole of her life, never travelled either by omnibus or railway, and was never more than 15 miles from her house.'

The cemetery was abandoned by the Abney Park Cemetery Company over 25 years ago, and was bought by the London Borough of Hackney. The council ignored it for the next twenty years, but luckily for us the result of this benign neglect was that it allowed the cemetery to develop into an 'urban forest'. The other side of that coin was a considerable amount of unchecked vandalism.

Nowadays, the Friends of Abney Park have a superb volunteer system which helps to maintain the grounds as a magnificent piece of north London parkland. The South Lodge also serves as a welcoming Visitor Centre with plenty of study materials to use, and books, postcards and posters for sale.

Notable Residents:

General William Booth *(1829-1912)* & **Catherine Booth** *(1829-1890)*– founders of the Salvation Army; **Dr Isaac Watts** *(1674-1748)* – theologan; **Frank C. Bostock** *(1866-1912)* – menagerist; **Rev Dr Thomas Binney** *(1798-1874)* – anti-slavery campaigner; **James Braidwood** *(1800-61)* – pioneering fire-fighter; **James Bronterre O'Brien** *(1805-1864)* – Irish Chartist leader; **Mary Hillum** *(1759-1864)*– see above.

Other names to look out for:

Sir Charles Reed *(1819-81)* – Hackney's first MP; **William Hone** *(1780-1842)* – Nonconformist bookseller; **Henry Vincent** *(1813-78)* – militant Chartist leader; **Mary Hillum** *(1759-1864)*– notable local; **Joanna Vassa** *(1795-1857)* – daughter of Olaudah Equiano, 'The African'.

East Finchley Cemetery (St Marylebone) (1854)

East End Road, East Finchley, N2 0RZ
Tel: 020 8567 0913
Transport: Finchley Central or East Finchley LU (then bus);
  Bus 143, 143A stop directly outside the entrance
Open: Mon-Fri 8.30am-4.30pm,
  Sat-Sun & Bank Hols 11am-4pm

Formerly known as Newmarket Farm, St Marylebone Cemetery was founded in 1854, and contains 22,000 graves in its 47 acres, as well as a large lodge and chapel decorated in fine Gothic style. A beautifully maintained cemetery, it won its first Green Flag award in 2007.

The wealth of the area in the late 19th and early 20th centuries resulted in some especially flamboyant monuments and sculptures. As you walk from the main entrance, don't miss the homoerotic sight of an angel hovering over a blue bronze, bare-chested muscular blacksmith. Above is a fine bust of the engineer **Sir Peter Nicol Russell** *(1816-1905)*, who made his fortune in Australia and helped fund the Sydney School of Engineering.

Opposite from Sir Russell's monument is the more modest grave of **Keith Blakelock** *(1945-85)*. Blakelock was the police officer murdered during the riots on the Broadwater Farm estate in Tottenham in 1985, a crime that remains a source of controversy as the man initially convicted was acquitted in 2003.

Further along Cypress Avenue look out for the stone angel which is a little obscured by a large yew tree. This marks the grave of famous music hall comedian William Henry Crump, better known as **Harry Champion** *(1865-1942)*. Further along Cypress Avenue take a right on Yew Avenue to find the grave of book illustrator **William Heath Robinson** *(1872-1944)*, best known for his intricate and impractical inventions. Take the narrow path just opposite Champion's grave to see on your left a large cross with a capital P at its centre marking the resting place of illustrator **Sidney Paget** *(1860-1908)*, famous for his illustrations of Conan Doyle's Sherlock Holmes stories. At the end of the path turn left and staight ahead you will find the grave of sculptor **Edward Onslow Ford** *(1852-1901)* whose only London statue is to Sir Rowland Hill near Postman's Park. Ford's grave is worthy of note for the fine laurel wreath made of bronze which sits upon his plain stone tablet, looking almost organic in its weathered condition. Follow the curve to the right to find a grand column upon which sits a globe, marking the resting place of explorer and naturalist, **Henry Walter Bates** *(1825-92)*. During his exploration of the Amazon, Bates discovered thousands of species and his work helped confirm Darwin's evolutionary theories. Further along is the imposing bronze relief on a large stone plinth marking the resting place of composer and professor of music, **Sir Henry Rowley Bishop** *(1786-1855)*.

Like Henry Bates, seen earlier, another supporter of Darwin was the eminent scientist **Thomas Henry Huxley** *(1825-95)*, who also coined the term 'agnostic', which he applied to his own ambivalent attitude to faith. His resting place is marked by a simple stone tablet that can be found along Central Avenue under an oak tree.

Close by is the grave of **Melanie Appleby** *(1966-90)*. She was just 23 when she succumbed to cancer, three years after she and her sister Kim got to number one in the UK pop charts with 'Respectable'. 'Mel & Kim' had a further three top ten hits before Mel became ill. Her grave is on the west side of Central Avenue, and features a bed of blue stones.

At the central crossroads, on West Avenue, look out for the stunning tomb for 'Australian colonist' **Thomas Skarratt Hall** *(1836-1903)*. It consists of a large grey and pink granite sarcophagus, apparently modelled on the tomb of Napoleon Bonaparte, which lies in Les Invalides in Paris. Originally there were four bronze angels at each corner but these were stolen in 1989.

Behind bushes on Central Avenue can be found the grave of **Alfred Harmsworth, Lord Northcliffe** *(1865-1922)*, who established the Daily Mail newspaper. His grave is a relatively plain, flat white slab surrounded by red flowers. He lies close to his brother and fellow newspaper magnate **Lord Rothermere** *(1868-1940)*.

At the junction with Rosemary Avenue and East Avenue is the resting place of legendary conductor **Leopold Stokowski** *(1882-1977)*, whose unique claim to fame is that it is his hand that Mickey Mouse shakes at the start of Fantasia. His monument is a plain greying stone bearing the words 'Music is the voice of the All'.

Notable Residents:

Sir Peter Nicol Russell *(1816-1905)* – engineer; **Keith Blakelock** *(1945-85)* – police officer; **Harry Champion** *(1865-1942)* – comedian; **William Heath Robinson** (1872-1944) – illustrator; **Sidney Paget** (1860-1908) – illustrator; **Edward Onslow Ford** (1852-1901) – sculptor; **Henry Walter Bates** (1825-92) – naturalist and explorer; **Sir Henry Rowley Bishop** (1786-1855) – composer; **Thomas Henry Huxley** (1825-95) – scientist; **Melanie Appleby** (1966-90) – pop singer; **Thomas Skarratt Hall** (1836-1903) – colonist; **Alfred Harmsworth Lord Northcliffe** (1865-1922) and **Lord Rothermere** (1868-1940) – press barons; **Leopold Stokowski** (1882-1977) – conductor.

Golders Green Crematorium (1902)

62 Hoop Lane, NW11 7NL
Tel: 020 8455 2374
www.crematorium.eu or www.londongardensonline.org
Transport: Golders Green LU (then 5 mins walk); Bus H2, 82,
113, 210
Open: Daily 9am-6pm (Apr-Oct), 9am-4pm (Nov-Mar)

London's first crematorium was built in 1902 when it became abundantly clear that the crematorium at the vast Brookwood Cemetery that began business in 1885 was not going to be large enough to meet Londoners increasing demand for cremation.

Cremation had been made legal only in 1884 and Golders Green quickly became the place where those in the media and arts chose to bid their last farewell, a fact reflected in the long list of celebrated figures whose names can be found here.

Almost 300,000 cremations have taken place in Golders Green, far more than at any other crematorium in Britain. By 1930, over a quarter of all UK cremations were carried out here, though the proportion has steadily dropped and nowadays around 3,500 souls a year are cremated at Golders Green. Its 12 acres feature superb memorial gardens, extensive columbaria and impressive water features.

Upon entry, turn left or right to see walls glistening with memorial tablets covering every spare inch. Take some time to cast an eye over them and every so often a familiar name will leap out. Golders Green is the place to go after-life star-spotting. From the acting world, the genius of comic actor **Peter Sellers** (1925-80)– here with his doting mother – is preserved beneath a rose bush (look for #39802), with an accompanying plaque on the wall behind reading 'Life is a state of mind. With ever loving memories, Peter Sellers'. Apparently, Sellers visited the crematorium just days before his sudden death from a heart attack in July 1980 – did he have a premonition? Fans of the man may want to stop by his former home in Muswell Hill Road which bears a plaque.

Elsewhere, look out for comedy actresses **Joyce Grenfell** *(1910-79)* and **Yootha Joyce** *(1927-80)*. Rock legends **Keith Moon** *(1946-78)* of The Who and elfin superstar **Marc Bolan** *(1947-77)* checked in within a year of each other in the late 70s – one from a drug overdose, the other a car crash. Bolan's rosebush is quite easy to find when it is in flower - just take the left path and look for the first white rosebush. The plaque reads 'much loved and missed by his fans and all those whose lives he touched'.

Writers are plentiful too. **Joe Orton** *(1933-67)* was cremated here in 1967. His ashes were combined with those of the man who'd murdered him – his lover Kenneth Halliwell – and spread in the Garden of Remembrance. The various plaques and tablets tell all kinds of stories from London's artistic and political history, not only of the famous but also the worthy and unsung. Inscriptions like 'Mike Cohen (1935-2002), fighter against fascism' tell us much about what someone achieved in their life, in just a few words.

Indie music fans may want to seek out music hall star **Cicely Courtneidge** *(1893-1980)*, whose name may be unfamiliar but whose voice is known to many as that which opens the track 'The Queen Is Dead' by the Smiths – an album that also features the song 'Cemetry Gates' (yes, that's a deliberate misspelling – any comments to Morrissey, please).

The Ernest George Mausoleum is the larger of two stark columbaria, and contains the ashes of the great psychoanalyst **Sigmund Freud** *(1856-1939)* in a Greek vase. This columbarium has five levels with a sea of urns and plaques to peruse. You can easily locate the urn of legendary ballerina **Anna Pavlova** *(1881-1931)*, draped in a pair of pink ballet shoes against the wall at ground level. A few minutes away up the hill a blue plaque marks the 'Ivy House', her home from 1911 until her death in 1931.

There are two impressively large mausolea on the east side – the Wren-style, brick-built Martin Smith Mausoleum and the Philipson Mausoleum. The latter is a temple-like circular structure designed by Sir Edwin Lutyens, the man responsible for much of the fine architecture around Golders Green itself.

Notable Residents:

Peter Sellers *(1925-80)* – comedian and actor; **Joyce Grenfell** *(1910-79)* – actor; **Yootha Joyce** *(1927-80)* – actor; **Keith Moon** *(1946-78)* – The Who's drummer; **Marc Bolan** *(1947-77)* – glam-rock legend; **Joe Orton** *(1933-67)* – playwright; **Cicely Courtneidge** *(1893-1980)* – music hall star; **Sigmund Freud** *(1856-1939)* – father of modern psychoanalysis; **Anna Pavlova** *(1881-1931)* – ballerina.

Other names to look out for:

Bram Stoker *(1847-1912)* – author of Dracula; **Enid Blyton** *(1897-1968)* – children's author; **Isaac Pitman** *(1813-97)* – inventor of shorthand; **Shiva Naipaul** *(1945-85)* – novelist; **Ronnie Scott** *(1927-96)* – jazz tenor saxophonist and jazz club owner.

Hampstead Cemetery (1876)

Fortune Green Road, West Hampstead NW6 1DR
Tel: 020 7527 8300
www.thefriendsofhampsteadcemetery.com
Transport: West Hampstead LU/Rail (5 min walk);
　　Bus 139, 328, C11, 82, 13
Open: Mon-Fri 7.30am-8.30pm (May-Jul); 7.30am-8pm (Aug);
　　7.30am-6.30pm (Mar & Sep); 7.30am-6pm (Oct); 7.30am-5pm
　　(Feb); 7.30am-4pm (Nov-Jan); Sat opens 9am, Sun & Bank
　　Holidays opens 10am

Hampstead Cemetery is located where West Hampstead meets
the Finchley Road, the locality that surrounds it goes by the
hopeful name of Fortune Green. Its 26 acres are designed in the
Egyptian style with no shortage of floral decoration. The broad
main drive runs very straight up to the twin Gothic-style chapels.
Both are listed buildings, and in front of them stands an entry
lodge made of Kentish ragstone and Bath stone.

Money received from the Heritage Lottery has gone a long
way to helping restore these buildings, as well as funding
road improvements and new landscaping. The main pathway
bisects the cemetery and leads from Fortune Green through to
Cricklewood, and is a good thoroughfare for walking towards
Paddington Old Cemetery (see page 72).

Entering from Fortune Green Road, the first extraordinary
sight is the bizarre bronze urn with a snake wrapped around it,
commemorating the poet **Arthur Frankau** *(1849-1904)*. Literary
folk feature heavily at Hampstead. A giant tomb for Henry
Stevens immortalises him as a 'lover of books', while you may have
to crouch almost to ground level to seek out the wonderful stone
sculpture of an open book with a disembodied hand for the writer
James Howard Wellard.

On the main path , where it crosses the pathway to
Cricklewood, is the tomb of the **Grand Duke Michael Mikhailovich**
(1861-1929) of Russia. A Romanov by birth, he escaped the Russian
revolution and certain execution by chance. After marrying below

his social rank in 1891, he was exiled from Russia and spent the rest of his life living in England and France.

Most of the best memorials are just off the main paths. At the top of the slope is the amazing 1929 replica of a church pipe organ (complete with bench) for Charles Barritt. From there, looking eastwards, the visitor can see the imposing Bianchi monument featuring a bright white effigy of a beautiful winged angel.. Dating from the 1930s, it commemorates the early death of the opera singing wife of an Italian restaurateur. On the left is carved a touching scene of the Bianchi family, sitting on a bench, cradling their infant son. Probably the most famous name here is **Joseph Lister** *(1827-1912)*, the man who pioneered antiseptic. He can be found in a pale granite sarcophagus, just in front of a representation of a First World War soldier.

Take some time to find two stars who died young – jockey **Fred Archer** *(1857-86)*, a five-times Derby winner who committed suicide aged 29 and the plain marble stone to mark **Dennis Brain** *(1921-57)*, a prodigy of the French horn, whose passion for fast cars led to an untimely curtain call at just 36. There is also the curious tale of **Florence Upton** *(1873-1921)*. A local girl, she turned to writing and illustrating children's books to escape financial difficulties, and decided to bring her old stash of dolls to life – the Golliwogg being the most famous and controversial of her creations.

Notable Residents:
Arthur Frankau *(1849-1904)* – poet; **Grand Duke Michael Mikhailovich** *(1861-1929)* – Russian royal; **Joseph Lister** *(1827-1912)* – surgeon and pioneer of antiseptics; **Fred Archer** *(1857-86)* – jockey, Derby winner;**Dennis Brain** *(1921-57)* – musician; **Charlotte Mew** *(1869-1928)* – tragic poet; **Florence Upton** *(1873-1921)* – children's author.

Other names to look out for :
Marie Lloyd *(1870-1922)* – music hall star; **Sir Tom O'Brien** *(1900-70)* – TUC president; **Ronald Fraser** *(1930-97)* – comedy actor.

Hendon Cemetery & Crematorium

(1899, crematorium added 1922)

Holders Hill Road, NW7 1NB
Tel: 020 8359 3370
www.barnet.gov.uk/cremation
Transport: Mill Hill East LU (then 240 southbound); Bus 240
Open: Daily 8.30am-4.30pm (Oct-Feb), 8.30am-5.30pm (Mar-
  Apr), 8.30am-7pm (May-Sep)

The architectural style at Hendon is an unusual mixture of black and white mock Tudor – much like the houses built in the 1920s in the area – and perpendicular Gothic, surfaced with knapped flint. The cemetery itself is fairly large, covering an area of 40 acres, and lending a very rural feel to what is a popular residential area.

Look inside the cloistered chapel to admire the large terracotta reredos – an ornamented, painted wall behind the altar – by Cantagalli, featuring a copy of Luca Della Robbia's 'Resurrection' from the cathedral in Florence.

Once outside the atmosphere is rather rustic, helped by the stream which traverses the site and which is crossed by several bridges. One of the grandest sights is the white mausoleum for Lord Marks. The unusually large number of bed-like graves with pillows is another distinctive feature of Hendon cemetery.

Plots devoted to citizens from Russia, Switzerland (see the monument marked 'Union Helvetia') and Greece (look out for the stepped tomb showing beautifully coloured scenes from Greek history) reflect the area's diverse population over the years. The large Japanese enclosure is lined with firs and cherry trees and dates from 1936; in early springtime it is particularly beautiful with hanami, or cherry blossom.

Notable Residents:

Edwin Mullins *(1848-1907)* – sculptor; **Frederick Bolton** *(1851-1920)* – ship owner; **Isaac Lodge** *(1866-1923)* – soldier.

Highgate Cemetery
West & East (1839 & 1854)

Highgate Cemetery, Swains Lane, N6 6PJ
Tel: 020 8340 1834
Email: info@highgatecemetery.org
www.highgatecemetery.org
Transport: Archway LU (then bus to Waterlow Park);
   Bus 143, 210, 271 (then 5 minutes walk through park)
East Cemetery open: Mon-Fri 10am-5pm (Mar-Oct) (last entry
   4.30pm), Mon-Fri 10am-4pm (Nov-Feb) (last entry 3.30pm),
   open 10am weekends
Admission: £4 (Adults), Children under 18 and members free
West Cemetery (guided tours only): Mon-Fri 11am & 1.45pm
   (prebooking required), weekend tours half-hourly 10.30am-
   4pm (Mar-Oct), 10.30am-3pm (Nov-Feb) (no advance booking
   required, tickets are sold on a first come first served basis)

Highgate is probably the best-known of London's cemeteries – a
Grade II listed park and a truly enchanting oasis of calm in the heart of
north London. Its vast and atmospheric 37 acres are probably most
famous for being home to **Karl Marx** *(1818-83)*. His mammoth bust
looks out in stoney silence over a small community of left-leaning
thinkers and activists who have collonised this corner of Highgate. In
2019 right wing activists vandalised his grave, which only serves to
emphasise Marx's importance to current political struggles.

The early 19th century was a time when burial conditions in
London became intolerable. The decision was taken to create seven
private cemeteries within the periphery of the city. Under the
guidance of architect Stephen Geary, Highgate's West Cemetery was
thus opened in 1839, the East Cemetery following in 1854. Since
then an estimated 173,000 names have been engraved on 53,000
headstones, at least 850 of which are notable. Today the Cemetery is
managed by the Friends of Highgate Cemetery. The East Cemetery
can be explored independently for a modest fee, while the West .can
only be visited as part of a guided tour.

The West Cemetery

Although the West Cemetery can usually only be seen as part of a guided tour, there is still a chance of making your own itinerary of sorts if you keep your eyes peeled.

Just a few footsteps into the West Cemetery's main entrance and the first notable resident becomes evident – record-breaking 19th-century coachman **James William Selby** *(1844-88)*, accompanied by a whip and an inverted set of horseshoes, an indication of how highly he was regarded. Just a little further up the path is a modest grave that is nonetheless remarkable. This marks the resting place of Russian dissident **Alexander Litvinenko** *(1962-2006)* who was poisoned by KGB agents using polonium-210. His grave is unique because of the lead coffin used to prevent any danger of radiation.

If you are able to take a detour and wander around the crescent to your right, you will soon come across the deceptively plain plot of the **Rossetti family** of poets, painters and scholars. Following the shaded woodland path rightwards, the exquisite Egyptian Avenue then comes into view to the left. The Victorians were endlessly fascinated by all things Egyptian, as evidenced by the British Museum and countless contemporaneous books. The avenue's entrance is breathtaking with obelisks and columns paving the way to a series of marvellous family vaults.

Also influenced by Egyptian (as well as the Gothic) styles, is the Circle of Lebanon which surrounds a magnificent, towering 300-year-old Cedar of Lebanon tree. The Circle is a perfectly curved pathway featuring tombs, vaults and winding paths dug deep into the hillside. The adjoining vaults resemble nothing so much as a series of luxury garages for the departed. Restoration work here resulted in the Europa Nostra Award being received in 2000.

On the north side is a row of vast family vaults, with one in particular being of great interest. **Radclyffe Hall** *(1880-1943)* was one of the first, if not the first, women to overtly allude to lesbianism in modern literature and her most celebrated work

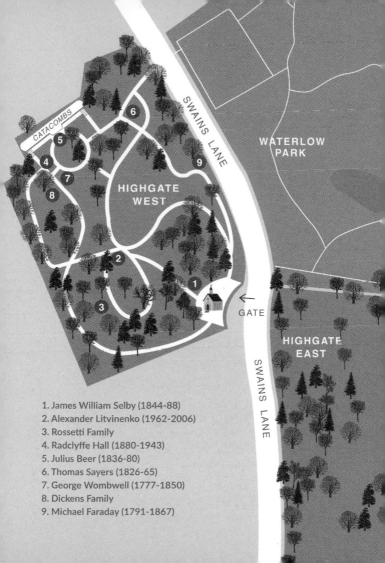

SWAINS LANE

WATERLOW
PARK

CATACOMBS

HIGHGATE
WEST

HIGHGATE
EAST

GATE

SWAINS LANE

1. James William Selby (1844-88)
2. Alexander Litvinenko (1962-2006)
3. Rossetti Family
4. Radclyffe Hall (1880-1943)
5. Julius Beer (1836-80)
6. Thomas Sayers (1826-65)
7. George Wombwell (1777-1850)
8. Dickens Family
9. Michael Faraday (1791-1867)

was banned from publication. Hall was a highly androgynous character who liked to be known as 'John'. Her novel *The Well of Loneliness* was published in 1928 and was a thinly veiled autobiography that showed lesbianism and female relationships in a positive and natural light. It caused all kinds of moral outrage at the time, in an uncanny echo of the treatment dished out to Oscar Wilde thirty years earlier.

Climbing steeply, we see the marvellously spooky terraced catacombs, all marking the wealth and importance of their occupants, before reaching the cemetery's highest point, at 1000 feet above sea level, to find the mausoleum of **Julius Beer** *(1836-80)*. Julius Beer was born into poverty in Frankfurt but became a wealthy banker in the City of London and later a newspaper tycoon. He and his family were not fully accepted by Victorian high society because of his Jewish origins and his having made his money in commerce. His revenge was this magnificent Italianate mausoleum, from where, Beer is able to lord it over his contemporaries and survey all London for eternity.

Returning towards Swains Lane, the grave of bare knuckle fighter **Thomas Sayers** *(1826-65)* is a fascinating curio, with his dog 'Lion' immortalised in marble and lying peacefully in front, guarding his memory. In the mid 19th century, Sayers was the Anthony Joshua of his age, a 'people's champion' for whom £3,000 was raised by his loyal fans to persuade him to retire after a punishing 42-round, two-hour fight against American champion John C Heenan. The theme of animals guarding the master's grave is not unique to Mr Sayers – check out the amazing sleeping lion on the tomb of **George Wombwell** *(1777-1850)*, legendary travelling animal showman who made his fortune introducing the Victorian public to exotic fauna. One resident who owes his fortune to the British love of dogs is **Charles Cruft** *(1852-1938)*, founder of the eponymous dog show, although his grave is a simple one, without the adornment of any kind of hound.

To the rear of the cemetery, running parallel to Swains Lane, is a relatively spartan area of unconsecrated ground, housing people whose sects were not recognized by the Church of England. An ordinary peaked monument commemorates scientist and electrical pioneer **Michael Faraday** *(1791-1867)* right by the north wall.

Cricket lovers should look out for the large Doric column upon a stone plinth with a shield relief carving of cricket bats and bowled out stumps that mark the tomb of legendary cricketer **F. W. Lillywhite** *(1792-1854)*. Lillywhite introduced 'roundarm' bowling to the professional game and acquired the moniker *Non Pareil* for his skilful application of the new technique. A simple engraved stone pavement marks the resting place of magician **David Devant** *(1868-1941)*. Little known today, Devant is widely regarded as one of the great magicians and invented several classic magic tricks that are still practiced to this day.

Crosses and angels line the paths as the overgrown weeds stretch over the grey marble. It is impossible not to notice the sheer wildness of this particular area, with butterflies, all manner of birds and even urban foxes roaming the scene. It is a wildness that makes the cemetery unique in London.

West Cemetery – Notable Residents:

James William Selby *(1844-88)* – coachman; **Alexander Litvinenko** *(1962-2006)* – KGB/FSB officer; **Rossetti Family** – artists, poets and scholars; **Radclyffe Hall** *(1880-1943)* – author; **Julius Beer** *(1836-80)* – proprietor of *The Observer*; **Thomas Sayers** *(1826-1865)* – bareknuckle boxer; **George Wombwell** *(1777-1850)* – managerist; **Charles Cruft** *(1852-1938)* – founder of the famous dog show; **Michael Faraday** *(1791-1867)* – chemist and electrical pioneer; **F. W. Lillywhite** *(1792-1854)* – cricketer, inventor of 'roundarm' bowling; **David Devant** *(1868-1941)* – magician.

Thomas Sayers

WATERLOW PARK

HIGHGATE WEST

GATE

McRUSSELL'S PATH

TOP ROAD

MAIN ROAD

SHAW'S PATH

KENDALL'S PATH

DISSENTER'S PATH

BACK ROAD

BOTTOM ROAD

HIGHGATE EAST

SWAINS LANE

DOG'S HEAD PATH

CHESTER ROAD

1. Thomas Pocklington (1860-1935)
2. Bruce Reynolds (1931-2013)
3. William Foyle (1885-1963)
4. Ralph Richardson (1902-83)
5. Max Wall (1908-90)
6. Corin Redgrave (1939-2010)
7. Alan Sillitoe (1928-2010)
8. Douglas Adams (1952-2001)
9. George Eliot (1819-80)
10. Malcolm McLaren (1946-2010)
11. .Jeremy Beadle (1948-2008)
12. Karl Marx (1818-83)
13. Paul Foot (1937-2004)
14. Eric Hobsbawn (1917-2012)

The East Cemetery

Open daily, and still very much a working burial ground, the East Cemetery is a maze of gently undulating pathways that form a crescent shape from the entrance in Swains Lane. On the left as you enter stand three stunning mausolea, the most inspiring being the Gothic splendour of social welfare pioneer **Thomas Pocklington's** *(1860-1935)* tomb. Close by is the striking death mask of great train robber **Bruce Reynolds** *(1931-2013)*, the frail octagenarian features bear little resemblance to Reynolds in his 1960s heyday.

Shortly ahead we come across **William Foyle** *(1885-1963)* of bookshop fame, and continuing along the central path we encounter theatrical luminaries **Sir Ralph Richardson** *(1902-1983)* and comedian **Max Wall** *(1908-90)* set among roughly-hewn gravestones. Sir Ralph's grave is an impeccably white slab that bears the words 'In treasured and tender memory', testimony to one of Britain's most acclaimed theatre actors, whose career included *Macbeth* at the Old Vic and Hollywood blockbuster *Rollerball*. A few minutes further on is the huge stone piano of Harry Thornton, minus its lid unfortunately. Thornton was a concert pianist who entertained troops during World War I, and later died in the 'flu epidemic of 1918.

The actor and political campaigner **Corin Redgrave** *(1939-2010)* has a simple gravestone. Nearby is the grave of author **Alan Sillitoe** *(1928-2010)* who wrote over forty novels and short stories but was best known for his early working-class dramas *Saturday Night and Sunday Morning* and *Loneliness of the Long Distance Runner*. **Douglas Adams** *(1952-2001)*, was a less prolific but equally successful author of *Hitchhikers Guide to the Gallery*.

Make a swift right and on the right lies Mary Ann Evans, better known as **George Eliot** *(1819-1880)*, author of *Middlemarch*, *The Mill on the Floss* and *Silas Marner*, and the most famous example of the Victorian phenomenon of a woman writing under a male pseudonym.

2010 saw the arrival in Highgate East of **Malcolm McLaren** *(1946-2010)*, the inimitable pop music impresario, situationist and all-round media figure. He is best known for managing the Sex Pistols in the late 1970s. His funeral parade brought traffic to a standstill in Camden Town, the coffin bearing the contemporaneous phrase 'Cash from Chaos'. His gravestone features a large, brown 'MM' motif with the words 'Malcolm Was Here' prominent. A close neighbour of McLaren is **Jeremy Beadle** *(1948-2008)* who presented popular television shows such as *You've Been Framed*. He was renowned for his general knowledge and his grave features a library of stone books.

For many the highlight of a visit to the East Cemetery is the imposing, stern-faced bust of **Karl Marx** *(1818-1883)* that hoves into view as you round the next bend. Marx looms over a steep, banked hill like a teacher facing a classroom, the hill featuring several leading communist figures from, amongst other places, Iraq, Israel, and South Africa. The monument reads, 'Workers of All Lands Unite – The Philosophers have only interpreted the world in various ways – The point however is to change it.' Not far away, is the grave of Marxist sociologist, **Ralph Miliband** *(1924-1994)* who is also the father of politicians David and Ed. The author and journalist **Paul Foot** *(1937-2004)* lies just across from Marx and behind him is the Marxist historian, **Eric Hobsbawn** *(1917-2012)*.

East Cemetery – Notable Residents:

Thomas Pocklington *(1860-1935)* – philanthropist; **Bruce Reynolds** *(1931-2013)* – great train robber; **William Foyle** *(1885-1963)* – founder of 'Foyles' bookshop; **Ralph Richardson** *(1902-1983)* – actor; **Max Wall** *(1908-90)* – comedian; **Corin Redgrave** *(1939-2010)* – actor and political activist; **Alan Sillitoe** *(1928-2010)* – author; **Douglas Adams** *(1952-2001)* – author; **George Eliot** *(1819-1880)* – author; **Malcolm McLaren** *(1946-2010)* – pop music impresario; **Jeremy Beadle** *(1948-2008)* – television presenter; **Karl Marx** *(1818-1883)* – political philosopher; **Ralph Miliband** *(1924-1994)* – Marxist and sociologist; **Paul Foot** *(1937-2004)* – journalist and author; **Eric Hobsbawn** *(1917-2012)* – historian.

WORKERS OF ALL LANDS

UNITE

KARL MARX

JENNY VON WESTPHALEN

Hoop Lane Cemetery (1897)

Hoop Lane, Golders Green, NW11 7NJ
020 8455 2569
www.hooplanecemetery.org.uk
Open: Sun-Thurs 8.30am-4.45pm, Fri 8.30am-3.45pm

Since its opening in 1897 this cemetery has met the needs of both the Reform and Sephardi Jewish communities. From the main entrance a central path divides the West London Synagogue burial ground on the left from the distinctive horizontal graves of the Spanish and Portuguese Sephardi community.

All the notable names are to be found in the West London Synagogue cemetery. Close to the entrance is the resting place of the screen writer **Jack Rosenthal** *(1931-2004)*, known for his humorous take on North London jewish life *Bar Mitzvah Boy* and the screenplay for the film *Yentl*, starring Barbara Streisand. Close by is the grave of British Reform rabbi **Hugo Gryn** *(1930-1996)* who was a popular contributor to BBC Radio 4's *Thought for the Day*. From here you can see the white marble grave of writer, **Erich Segal** *(1937-2010)*, best known for his novel *Love Story*, which was adapted into an Oscar winning film. Further along the central avenue in row 42 is the grave of the renowned agony aunt **Marjorie Proops** *(1911-96)*. Any person who has struggled to pass their driving test should seek out the pink granite tomb of Leslie Hore-Belisha, **Baron Hore-Belisha** *(1893-1957)*, who as Minister of Transport in the 1930s introduced the driving test. The most famous person here is the cellist **Jacqueline du Pré** *(1945-87)*, who enjoyed great success before multiple sclerosis ended her career at just 28. After many years of illness she eventually died, aged 42, in October 1987.

Notable Residents:

Jack Rosenthal *(1931-2004)* – playwright; **Hugo Gryn** *(1930-1996)* – Rabbi; **Erich Segal** *(1937-2010)* – novelist; **Marjorie Proops** *(1911-96)* – journalist; **Baron Hore-Belisha** *(1893-1957)* – politician; **Jacqueline du Pré** *(1945-1987)* – cellist.

Mill Hill Cemetery (New Paddington) (1936)

Milespit Hill, NW7 2RR
Tel: 020 8567 0913
www.westminster.gov.uk/millhill-cemetery
Transport: Mill Hill East LU
(then bus 221 or 240 towards Edgware)
Open: Mon-Fri 8.30am-6pm, Sat-Sun & Bank Hols 11am-4pm
(Mar-Oct); Mon-Fri 8.30am-4.30pm, Sat-Sun & Bank Hols
8.30am-4.30pm (Nov-Feb)

In 1923 the Borough of Paddington realized that the cemetery in Willesden Lane was almost full. Plans were made to build a 26 acre site which had to be within eight miles of Paddington Town Hall – Mill Hill, just managed to fit the bill.

The cemetery is one of London's finest with regard to Second World War memorials and is of particular interest to visitors from the Netherlands. The brick chapel, resembling a mini version of the Tate Modern, leads to a plot of neatly lined war graves surrounded by a clipped yew hedge, administered by the Commonwealth War Graves Commission, next to a Royal British Legion memorial. RAF motifs dominate due to the proximity of what was once Hendon aerodrome (now the RAF Museum).

In the north of the cemetery, the Dutch National War Memorial is the main feature of the Netherlands Field of Honour, a half-acre plot containing the graves of 254 Dutch naval servicemen and women killed during World War II. The central memorial is a bronze figure of a dying man by the artist Von Kralingen. The plot was opened in 1965 by Prince Bernhard of the Netherlands. To find these graves turn left at the entrance, keep walking until you see a group of neatly set out white headstones in rows of eight.

Just opposite the Dutch war graves can be found the resting place of legendary rock 'n' roll star **Billy Fury** *(1941-83)*. Born Ronald Wycherley in Liverpool in 1941, he was one of the few home-grown stars worthy of the title 'the British Elvis', and had a succession of hits such as 'Halfway To Paradise' in the early 1960s. He died in 1983 after a life blighted by heart problems. His marble headstone is heart-shaped, with flowers and cards always surrounding it.

Moving to the south of the cemetery, we come across civilian memorials to the residents of Paddington and nearby Hendon who lost their lives during the Second World War. Also here is **John Laing** *(1879-1978)*, the founder of the building company that bears his name, and who was also president of the London Bible College, and First World War hero **Michael O'Leary** *(1890-1961)*. O'Leary was the first member of the Irish Guards to be awarded a VC, which he won for his one man assault upon a German machine gun position in Cuinchy, France in February 1915. Unlike many of his comrades he lived to receive his VC and became a Major in the Second World War. In this area (Plot B1) look out for the unremarkable plaque marking the resting place of 'Writer and Bohemian', **Julian Maclaren-Ross** *(1912-64)*. His novels and short stories capture his dissolute life in post-war Fitzrovia, which ended prematurely at the age of just 52 in a spiral of debt and alcoholism.

There is a designated 'quiet area', surrounded by a beautiful hedge, with a memorial stone in the centre commemorating a communal grave that contains the remains of those interred at the old St Mary's Paddington Green before it was cleared for the construction of the Westway. A wildflower meadow has been created on unused burial land, helping to enhance the rural feel of this cemetery, even though the M1 begins it's long journey north a short distance away. Look out too for the unusual and heart-warming small carving of an old lady sitting peacefully on a bench.

Notable Residents:
Billy Fury *(1941-83)* – rock'n'roll singer; **John Laing** *(1879-1978)* – builder and president of London Bible College; **Michael O'Leary** *(1890-1961)* – World War I hero; **Julian Maclaren-Ross** *(1912-64)* – author.

New Southgate Cemetery (1861)

Brunswick Park Road, N11 1JJ
Tel: 020 8361 1713
www.newsouthgatecemetery.co.uk
Transport: Arnos Grove LU, New Southgate Rail; Bus 34, 125,
    184, 251
Open: Mon-Fri 9am-5pm, Sat 9am-12noon

The gargoyles on the elaborate Gothic gateposts seem to chuckle mischievously as the visitor enters and begins to walk down the cemetery's heavily planted and landscaped drives. Unfortunately barely any trace remains of the railway terminus set up in the days when the cemetery's owners linked it to the Great Northern Railway at King's Cross, and coffins could be sent via a mile-long branch line from Colney Hatch.

Formerly known as the Great Northern Cemetery, New Southgate could well claim to be the cemetery that best represents the multi-culturalism of London with graves baring the names of people from across the globe and representing a wide variety of faiths.

New Southgate is very much a working cemetery but with limited land amid Southgate's surrounding urban sprawl, the owners persuaded parliament to pass *The New Southgate Cemetery Act* in 2017. The act permits the re-use of graves more than 75 years old to make way for new residents with major works in progress in some of the older parts of the cemetery. A stone to the right of the entrance reminds visitors that such upheavals are not new, as it commemorates the 129 coffins and 197 bones removed from St Michael Bassishaw in the City of London in 1897 following parochial restructuring.

One casualty of these changes is the imposing obelisk commemorating 19th-century Quakers which had fallen into disrepair and has recently been removed. One survivor is the simple tablet at the cemetery's entrance remembering 51 Germans killed at nearby Alexandra Palace while interned during the First World War. Continue down the main path into

the central circular area to find the modern-looking chapel and crematorium, and a war memorial. To the north-east, there is a section reserved for the use of Hendon Reform Synagogue.

Head left from the crematorium, and follow the path to the main attraction at New Southgate, the walled flower garden containing the grave of **Shoghi Effendi** (1896-1957), founder of the Baha'i faith. He died unexpectedly while visiting London in 1957, and lies in New Southgate because the rules of his faith dictated that the place of burial had to be within an hour of the actual place of death. Look out for the massive white marble column that supports a golden eagle sitting on a globe. Considered a sacred place by members of the Baha'i faith, the grave receives a steady flow of visitors. At night its shadowy silhouette can be seen from outside the cemetery.

New Southgate has one of the strongest links with local ethnic communities of any cemetery in London, which is evident in the colour and variety of graves and memorials on display. North London's Greek Cypriot community has had a huge impact on the cemetery, and a new Greek Orthodox area set up in 1998 was named after Reverend Kyriacou Petrou, an eminent local priest buried in the section. Flowers and petals can be seen everywhere. There is also a Caribbean and African section.

The new 'Virgin Mary' Roman Catholic area, opened in 1997, is surrounded by landscaped lawns and banks, and while the older sections contain predominantly Irish families, this newer section features names that suggest residents of Mediterranean or Polish origin.

Notable Residents:
Shoghi Effendi *(1896-1957)* – religious leader.

Paddington Old Cemetery (1855)

Willesden Lane, Kilburn, NW6 7SD
Transport: Kilburn LU, Brondesbury Park Rail; Bus 98
Open: Daily 9am-4pm (Jan-Feb & Nov-Dec), 9am-5pm (Oct),
    9am-6pm (Mar), 9am-7pm (Apr & Sep), 9am-8pm (May-Aug)

Kilburn is permanently on the verge of being London's latest 'up and coming' residential area, but until that comes to pass, the finest jewel in this area of London is Paddington Old Cemetery.

Opened in 1855, it provides a welcome 25 acre open space with 500 mature trees and formal bedding schemes and lawns. The paths follow a horseshoe shape and lead into wildlife areas with an enormous variety of wild flowers. It's very grassy and looks rather roomy for such an old cemetery. The centrepiece of the cemetery is two Grade II listed buildings – twin chapels built in the early 1850s and designed by Thomas Little, who was also responsible for the chapel at Nunhead. The style used here is 13th-century Gothic – with each chapel bearing a 'porte cochère' (covered entrance) and central belfry, linked by arches. Only one chapel however remains in use.

The cemetery has several impressive granite monuments, one of the finest being the skillfully carved and polished example for local mason John Cramb dating from 1902. Look out for architect **Edward Barry** *(1830-1880)*, who designed the Royal Opera House in Covent Garden, the temperance reformer **Jabez Burns** *(1805-1876)*, and three-times Derby winning jockey **Danny Maher** *(1881-1916)*. Born in Connecticut, Maher died at just 35 from consumption after years of starving himself to make racing weight – see also Fred Archer in Hampstead Cemetery (page 50).

Notable Residents:

Edward Barry *(1830-1880)* – architect; **Jabez Burns** *(1805-1876)* – temperance reformer; **Danny Maher** *(1881-1916)* – jockey.

St Pancras & Islington Cemetery (1877)

High Road, East Finchley, N2 9AG
Tel: 020 7527 8300
www.iccslondon.co.uk
Transport: East Finchley LU (10 min walk); Bus 263, 43, 134, 221
Open: Mon-Fri 7.30am-5pm (Feb-Nov), 7.30am-4pm (Dec-Jan),
    Weekends and Holidays opens 9am

The first publicly owned cemetery in London, St Pancras and Islington is also the largest. It is actually divided into two sections owned by Islington and Camden Councils, but under a long standing agreement is entirely run by Islington Council.

Old pinnacled Gothic railings stand at the eastern entrance to the vast 182 acre site. The original chapels designed by the esteemed architects Barnett and Birch contrast beautifully – one in decorated Gothic for the Anglicans, the other with a spectacular six-sided lantern for Dissenters. A hundred-foot spire rises up from the Anglican chapel and looks out over central London.

Moving further inwards (and indeed upwards, given the gradient) from the north-western entrance, you soon come across the spire-like World War II memorial. The neat angular rows of 191 identical, upright war graves stand to attention, and include some headstones commemorating Belgian casualties too.

St Pancras isn't just looming spires though – several of its quirkier inhabitants and their monuments see to that. There used to be a marvellously theatrical statue of the road-sweeper and original pearly king **Henry Croft** *(1861-1930)*, but persistent vandalism has led to its removal – there is still a photograph of the monument on the headstone. The effigy of Mr Croft is now on display in the Crypt of St Martin-in-the-Fields Church in Central London. The stone balloon of the pioneering aeronaut **Percival Spencer** *(1864-1913)* is in the process of repair. Nonetheless, the parachuting figure on the memorial to the 'famous Lyceum clown' **Harry Gardner** *(1871-1917)* remains, with the words 'Peace, Perfect Peace'.

In the south-east of the cemetery, and widely considered to be its finest monument, is a vast mausoleum erected for the German-Jewish industrial chemist **Ludwig Mond** *(1839-1909)*. This Greek style temple made of grey granite with vast Ionic columns was erected by his son **Alfred Moritz Mond, Baron Melchett** *(1868-1930)* who later formed Imperial Chemical Industries (ICI). Ludwig Mond was a man renowned for his philanthropy, and his collection of early Italian paintings is now in the National Gallery.

Take the narrow path to the left of the Mond mausoleum to find, set back amid undergrowth, the grave of painter **Ford Madox Brown** *(1821-93)*. Madox Brown was associated with the Pre-Raphaelites, but never shared their success, his talent was only fully appreciated after his death.

Reverse your steps and take the path to your right, at the path's apex you will find the fine stone tablet commemorating the actor **Edward William Elton** *(1794-1843)*. He had just finished a successful run at the Adelphi Theatre Edinburgh, when he boarded the ill-fated Pegasus steam ship which sank off rocks in the Firth of Forth. Of the 57 people on board only six survived. Elton's death inspired great public sympathy and the young Charles Dickens was among the notables involved in raising funds for the care of the actor's orphaned children.

Notable Residents:

Henry Croft *(1861-1930)* – road sweeper, original 'Pearly King'; **Percival Spencer** *(1864-1913)* – pioneering aeronaut; **Harry Gardner** *(1871-1917)* – Clown; **Ludwig Mond** *(1839-1909)* – industrialist; **Alfred Moritz Mond**, **Baron Melchett** *(1868-1930)* – industrialist; **Ford Madox Brown** *(1821-93)* – artist; **Edward William Elton** *(1794-1843)* – actor.

St Pancras Old Church

Pancras Road, NW1 1UL
Tel: 020 7424 0724
posp.co.uk/st-pancras-old-church
Open: Daily dawn till dusk

St Pancras Old Church faced a major reconfiguration in the 1860s to make way for the Midland Railway. The job of managing the exhumations and reburials was given to architect Arthur Blomfield and he delegated the task to his young assistant, one Thomas Hardy.

Hardy was to become one of the great novelists of the 19th century, penning classics such as *Tess of the D'Urbervilles* and *Jude the Obscure* and he applied this vivid imagination to the task at hand. He moved the displaced headstones to be arranged in pairs around the base of a large ash tree that still stands in the centre of the church yard today. The pattern of stones was probably striking at the time, but has become distorted over the years as the roots of the tree have forced themselves between the stones and created an uneven pattern that is slightly macabre as if the dead were trying to rise again.

Hardy was clearly affected by the work, as over 20 years later he penned the poem *The Levelled Churchyard (1880-1)*:

> *O passenger, pray list and catch*
> *Our sighs and piteous groans,*
> *Half stifled in this jumbled patch*
> *of wrenched memorial stones!*

> *We late-lamented, resting here,*
> *Are mixed to human jam,*
> *And each to each exclaim in fear,*
> *'I know not which I am!'*

One resident of St Pancras that does know their place is the renowned architect **Sir John Soane** *(1753-1837)*. The Soane Mausoleum was erected in 1816 to house Soane's wife Elizabeth

(1760-1815) and later became the family vault where Soane and his son lie. The tomb is a grand affair complete with cast iron railing to discourage people intruding on the family's privacy and is Grade I listed. Nikolaus Pevsner described it as an 'outstandingly interesting monument...extremely Soanesque with all his originality and all his foibles'. The central dome of the structure is said to have been the inspiration for Sir Giles Gilbert Scott's design for the K2 telephone box which can still be seen on the streets of London today.

A more modest grave marks the resting place of the feminist writer **Mary Wollstonecraft** *(1759-97)* and her philosopher husband **William Godwin** *(1756-1836)*. The graves remain but in 1851 the bodies were moved and re-interred with their daughter Mary Shelley in Bournemouth. The eminent sculptor **John Flaxman** *(1755-1826)* lies with his family under two large stone tablets that have become quite eroded over the years, unlike Flaxman's monument for Lord Nelson's tomb which can be seen in St Paul's Cathedral. The infamous thief-taker **Jonathan Wild** *(1683-1725)* was buried here following his execution at Tyburn but was later disinterred and is now on display at the Hunterian Museum.

Notable Residents:

Sir John Soane *(1753-1837)* – architect; **Mary Wollstonecraft** *(1759-97)* – author; **William Godwin** *(1756-1836)* – philosopher; **John Flaxman** *(1755-1826)* – sculptor; **Jonathan Wild** *(1683-1725)* – criminal.

Sir John Soane

Tottenham Cemetery (1858)

White Hart Lane/Church Lane, N17 8AT
Tel: 020 8363 8324
Transport: Seven Sisters LU (then bus 279 or 149),
    White Hart Lane Rail; Bus 279, 149, 121, W3
Open: Daily 7.30am-4.30pm

Opened in 1858, Tottenham Cemetery covers approximately 62 acres, with an East and a West Chapel both built in Gothic style. The most notable resident is probably **William Butterfield** *(1814-90)*, a Victorian church architect who designed his own family's plot complete with a medieval-style coffin tomb with a sculpted cross on the top. Butterfield is best remembered locally for having restored the nearby All Hallows church.

Walking along the winding path, which resembles a well-designed karting circuit, the chapels soon hove into view, shading the entrance to the Garden of Peace. The Garden of Peace covers about a quarter of the cemetery and is a marvellous example of how a cemetery can be transformed into a home for abundant wildlife. The centrepiece is a sizeable lake, fed by a natural spring, which is home to all kinds of flora and fauna.

The memorials at Tottenham are those of ordinary folk rather than of national icons. A winged angel on a cloud commemorates Bert Oakby who 'fell asleep' in May 1953 with a scroll bearing the message 'Some day, some time, we'll understand'. At least three family memorials feature homely-looking gates, such as the O'Sullivan tomb for William George (1937) who was 'Reunited' with Jane in 1968.

In 2008 the cemetery celebrated its 150th anniversary. Festivities included the Mayor of Haringey reactivating the waterfall at the cemetery's lake for the first time in 30 years.

Notable Residents:
William Butterfield *(1814-90)* – architect.

Tottenham Park Cemetery (1912)
inc. Western Synagogue Cemetery (1889)

Dodsley Place, 247 Montagu Road, N9 0EU
Tel: 07498 201225
www.tottenhamparkcemetery.co.uk
Transport: Edmonton Green Rail; Bus 192, 363
Open: Daily 10am-4pm

Tottenham Park is a cemetery of two halves. The main part is a medium-sized private burial ground dating from 1912 which is sited next to the older Edmonton Federation Cemetery run by the Western Synagogue.

The cemetery has a fairly uneventful history, being originally the last resting place for the majority of N18's poorest residents. At least until the late 1960s, when for some inexplicable reason it became a magnet for satanists, culminating in a violent desecration in 1968 complete with disturbed graves, corpses disinterred and even the odd impaling. Thankfully all that is long-forgotten.

The original brick Gothic chapel is now disused and derelict, with a block of 1960s flats obscuring the once pretty entrance from Montagu Road. Lime trees line the central drive though, and there is still a lot to see thanks to the bright colours and red crescents that denote Muslim burials.

Once the old working class deserted the area, the cemetery fell into disrepair. The Muslim community effectively saved Tottenham cemetery. It's now a colourful sea of arches, mini-minarets, freshly delivered flowers and lovingly tended graves. Some of the graves are heart-shaped, with enough flowers beside them to distress any hay fever sufferer.

Now privately owned, the cemetery has been maintained by the Friends of Tottenham Park Cemetery since the early 1990s and is now designated a Conservation Area. Thanks to their improvements, the cemetery is well worth a visit. One of the best changes is the creation of a series of stepped wooden trellises

with associated planting and seats to the right of the path leading towards the chapel.

The Western Synagogue was established in 1761 and the cemetery in Montagu Road opened in 1889. The main Western Cemetery is now in Cheshunt, a move in step with the Jewish migration northwards to Hertfordshire. The Western Marble Arch Synagogue, which replaced The Western Synagogue in 1991, now holds the records for the Montagu Road Cemetery. Visitors enter the cemetery through a set of elaborate ornamental iron gates that lead into a gravelled driveway, with some beautifully kept flowers in front of a square brick prayer hall. The hall itself is somewhat stark and does not exude the warmest of welcomes.

There's certainly plenty of marble and granite in evidence, and as with many Jewish cemeteries there are rows and rows of very uniform tall headstones. Two brick mausolea give the place some extra character, one of which is for a highly-esteemed Russian rabbi and dates from 1910.

Willesden New Cemetery (1891)

Franklyn Road, NW10 9TE
Transport: Dollis Hill LU; Bus 260, 266, 297
Open: Daily 9am-4pm (Jan-Feb & Nov-Dec), 9am-6pm (Mar),
    9am-7pm (Apr & Sep), 9am-8pm (May-Aug), 9am-5pm (Oct)

The name may suggest a new cemetery but in truth this facility
was opened more than a century ago, in 1891. The centrepiece
is the Willesden War Memorial, a tribute to local civilians who
perished in the Second World War. The cemetery is full of roses,
shrubs and mature trees that obscure the city beyond and add a
welcome dash of colour and vegetation to the area.

One granite monument poses a little exotic mystery. It is the
last resting place of 'Ernest Schwarz of the Kalahari', of whom
little is known beyond the fact that he died in 1928.

Wood Green Cemetery (1996)

Wolves Lane, N22 5DQ
Tel: 020 8363 8324
www.dignityfunerals.co.uk
Transport: Wood Green LU; Bus 121, W4, 144
Open: Daily 7.30am-4.30pm

Opened in 1996, Wood Green is small but charming. Naturally,
being recently built, it has a busy burial schedule, so visitors
should be sensitive to the working life of the cemetery.

The grounds are defined with pebble paths with flowering
trees and shrubs creating colour and depth. The cemetery very
much reflects the cosmopolitan nature of its local communities,
and these days features one of the finest Muslim sections of
any London cemetery. The Muslim influence is apparent in
the colourful, crescent-bearing plots. The effect is to give the
cemetery an exotic eastern flavour.

Wood Green Cemetery has acquired several Green Flag awards
over the years, recognising it as on of the best open spaces to be
enjoyed in Haringey.

Brompton Cemetery

West

Acton Cemetery (1895)

Park Royal Road, W3 6XA

Tel: 020 8825 6030

Transport: North Acton LU, Acton Rail; Bus 95, 260, 266, 440, 487

Open: Mon-Fri 8am-7.30pm (May-Aug), 8am-7pm (Apr & Sep),
    8am-5.30pm (Mar & Oct), 8am-4.30pm (Nov-Feb) – open 9am
    weekends

Acton has two chapels dating from 1895 built in conventional English Gothic style. With its well tended lawn, the cemetery is not really the place for plant or wildlife spotting. It does, however, have one or two worthwhile graves, all of which are concentrated around the chapel at the Park Royal Road entrance, where a map shows their location.

A granite cross, featuring an anchor framed in a wreath, commemorates **Albert Perry** *(1889-1915)*. Perry was one of 1,200 souls who died when the liner Lusitania was sunk off the coast of Ireland in May 1915 on its way to London from Perry's native New York. There's also an imposing angel pointing to the heavens above the final resting place of **George Temple** *(1892-1914)*, who was a pioneer aviator and the founder of the Temple Flying School at Hendon Aerodrome. Temple was killed when he crashed his plane during a flying display on the 25th January 1914. An unremarkable stone tablet marks the grave of **Sir Samuel Lewis** *(1843-1903)* the first mayor of Freetown, the third Sierra Leonean to qualify as a barrister and the first West African to be knighted. Acton is also the resting place of **Susan Mary Yeats** *(1841-1900)* who was the wife of artist John Butler Yeats and mother to the great poet William Butler Yeats. She had six children, four of whom became notable in their fields but little is known of her.

Notable Residents:

Albert Perry (1889-1915) – victim of the Lusitania sinking; **George Temple** (1892-1914) – aviator; **Sir Samuel Lewis** (1843-1903) – barrister; **Susan Mary Yeats** *(1841-1900)* – mother of WB Yeats.

Loving Memory
of
GEORGE LEE TEMPLE
C. INST. MECH. E. C. M. Y.
BORN 19 AUGUST 1892
HE WAS THE FIRST BRITISH AIRMAN
TO FLY UPSIDE DOWN
IN THIS COUNTRY 24 NOV 1913.
AND THE YOUNGEST TO FLY FROM

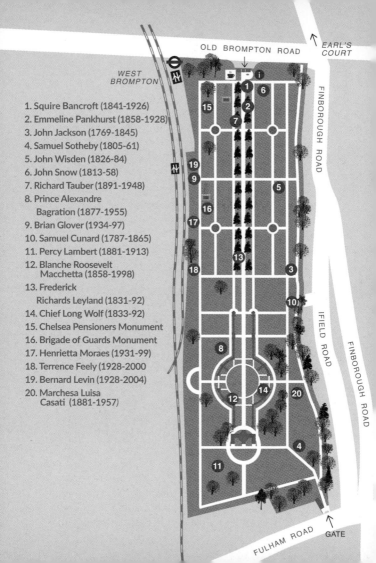

OLD BROMPTON ROAD

↑ EARL'S COURT

WEST BROMPTON

FINBOROUGH ROAD

IFIELD ROAD

FINBOROUGH ROAD

FULHAM ROAD

GATE

1. Squire Bancroft (1841-1926)
2. Emmeline Pankhurst (1858-1928)
3. John Jackson (1769-1845)
4. Samuel Sotheby (1805-61)
5. John Wisden (1826-84)
6. John Snow (1813-58)
7. Richard Tauber (1891-1948)
8. Prince Alexandre Bagration (1877-1955)
9. Brian Glover (1934-97)
10. Samuel Cunard (1787-1865)
11. Percy Lambert (1881-1913)
12. Blanche Roosevelt Macchetta (1858-1998)
13. Frederick Richards Leyland (1831-92)
14. Chief Long Wolf (1833-92)
15. Chelsea Pensioners Monument
16. Brigade of Guards Monument
17. Henrietta Moraes (1931-99)
18. Terrence Feely (1928-2000)
19. Bernard Levin (1928-2004)
20. Marchesa Luisa Casati (1881-1957)

Brompton Cemetery (1840)

Old Brompton Road, SW10 9UG
(South Gate off Fulham Road, North Gate off Old Brompton Road)
Tel: 020 7352 1201 (Chapel Office);
   020 7352 1201 (Friends of Brompton)
www.brompton-cemetery.org.uk
Transport: West Brompton LU & Overground; Bus 14, 74, C1
Open: Daily 7am-4pm (Winter), Daily 7am-8pm (Summer)

Brompton is the closest of the major cemeteries to the centre of London – just several stones' throws from Harrods, it is book-ended by the Brompton Road and Fulham Road and can be seen from the stands of Chelsea FC's Stamford Bridge ground.

The original 40 acres had a formal layout designed by Benjamin Baude, based on the plan of a vast cathedral, with a chapel in the middle unambiguously based on St Peter's Basilica in Rome. Built on land owned by Lord Kensington, it was extended in 1844 to provide access onto Fulham Road.

The original proposals turned out to be so expensive that the cemetery might not have survived had the government not agreed to purchase all the London cemeteries in 1850. That edict was repealed just two years later, but Brompton somehow escaped the bullet and as a consequence remains the only public cemetery under government control. It is now managed by the Royal Parks Agency under the Minister for Culture, Media and Sport.

The cemetery boasts some fantastic monuments among its 70,000 graves and is home to a surprising abundance of wildlife, including a variety of butterflies and unusual insects.

To access the cemetery from the entrance closest to West Brompton tube station, enter through the North Gate. The avenues lying ahead are straight, broad and seen from above conform to a grid system.

The grave of the distinguished, monocled actor **Squire Bancroft** *(1841-1926)* is one of the first to be seen on the left side of the central avenue. This is an odd memorial because it is the front façade of his now demolished mausoleum. It is a little-known fact that in his later years as a theatre owner, Bancroft coined the term 'matinees' for pre-evening performances.

Shortly afterwards we come across a statue that commemorates **Emmeline Pankhurst** *(1858-1928)*. As a teenager, she became passionate about the enfranchisement of women thanks to her liberal parents. The death of her husband in 1898 turned her passion into an obsession, leading to a three-month prison sentence in 1908 for a breach of the peace. A photograph of Pankhurst being seized by a policeman outside Buckingham Palace, is one of the iconic images of the 20th century.

Things changed with the onset of the First World War and Britain was forced to call upon women to do jobs formerly the responsibility of men. When peace was declared the government finally bowed to pressure and gave women the vote. Pankhurst herself stood for Parliament as a Conservative candidate, but eventually retired to the French Riviera. She died shortly before the passing of the 1928 Act that gave voting rights to disenfranchised men and most women. A short path leads up to her dignified monument, a celtic cross with an image of Christ – quite different from the towering statue of Pankhurst herself that stands close to the House of Lords in Westminster.

Halfway down the avenue is the beautiful **Frederick Leyland** *(1831-92)* monument. Designed by Edward Burne-Jones and resembling a small hut on pillars, it is widely considered to be the finest surviving pre-Raphaelite sculpture in London. Leyland was a patron of the arts and president of the National Telephone Company, and his gated tomb decorated with wild lilies is the kind of art that deserves a museum room of its own.

One of the most picturesque tombs is that of opera singer **Richard Tauber** *(1891-1948)*, a beautiful flower-laden grave. Tauber was born in Austria, started his career in Germany and soon became not only the most popular singer in 1930s 'Mittel Europa' but also a leading conductor and composer. Tauber's Jewish origins made him a target of Nazi Germany, and he fled to London where he continued performing until his death from cancer at just 56.

Frederick Leyland

A flat granite slab commemorates Canadian-born **Samuel Cunard** *(1787-1865)*, a pioneer of transatlantic steam travel, who established the Cunard Line in 1840. Actor and 'professional Yorkshireman' **Brian Glover** *(1934-97)* is commemorated by a stone set into the ground marked 'Wrestler, Actor, Writer', which succinctly sums up the three art forms in which he excelled. Best known for his role as the sports teacher in Ken Loach's classic film *Kes*, he also made memorable appearances in *Porridge* and *An American Werewolf in London*. He died of a brain tumour at just 63. Close by is the more recent grave of controversial journalist and commentator **Bernard Levin** *(1928-2004)*, who could have benefitted from Mr Glover's martial skills when thumped on live television by an angry husband enraged by Levin's acerbic criticism of his wife's acting. Further along is the resting place of **Henrietta Moraes** *(1931-99)* who was a model for both Lucian Freud and Francis Bacon and enjoyed a colourful and wild life among Soho's artist community. She died leaving her dachshund Max and a pile of unpaid bills. Also within this section is the grave of screenwriter **Terrence Feely** *(1928-2000)* who was responsible for popular television series such as *The Avengers*, *The Prisoner* and *The Saint*.

John Snow is one of the most important British figures in the history of medicine. He was the man who discovered that cholera was caused by contaminated water. As well as being the first doctor to use ether as an anaesthetic in England, he also administered chloroform to Queen Victoria as she gave birth to her son Leopold, an experience she is said to have described as 'soothing, quieting and delightful beyond measure'. In 1941 the Luftwaffe put paid to his tomb but in 1951 The Association of Anaesthetists replaced it with the current one – a bright white pedestal, topped by a draped urn.

One of the most well-known names in auctioneering is Sotheby's, and founder **Samuel Sotheby** *(1805-61)* can be found at Brompton, his tree-like monument featuring a circular motif of an embracing couple. Another instantly recognizable brand name whose founder lies at this cemetery, is Wisden.

Former player **John Wisden** *(1826-84)* established the famous *Cricketer's Almanac* a year after rheumatism forced him to give up the game, and his annual has continued to be published with relatively little alteration since 1864. His grave lay unmarked for a century but on the hundredth anniversary of his death in April 1984 a black headstone with a contemporary portrait of the great man was unveiled.

According to his tombstone, which is a broken column, motor racing pioneer **Percy Lambert** *(1881-1913)* was 'A modest friend, a fine gentleman and a thorough sportsman'. Like all good early racers, he met his demise at speed, on the track at Brooklands.

'Gentleman **John**' Jackson *(1769-1845)* was national boxing champion from 1795 to 1803 before opening a boxing academy in Bond Street whose old boys included Lord Byron and the Marquis of Queensberry himself. His monument is a giant sleeping lion atop a large tomb, paid for by a grateful London public. Nearby is the rather plain grave of **Prince Alexandre Bagration** *(1877-1955)*. His aristocratic ancestors lie in rather grander circumstances in Moscow, while Alexandre ended his days in London as an emigre from the Russian revolution.

Blanche Roosevelt Macchetta *(1858-1998)* was originally from Ohio but it took a move to Europe to make her famous. After studying music in London, she became the first American woman to sing Italian opera at Covent Garden. Her monument is a statue of a curly-haired woman clutching a rose.

One curio in the history of Brompton cemetery is the tale of the American Sioux Indian Chief, **Long Wolf** *(1833-92)*. A major figure in the Sioux wars of the 1870s, he was originally buried here after he succumbed to bronchial pneumonia whilst touring Europe with *Buffalo Bill's Wild West Show*. He was buried in London for over a century before his remains were finally returned home to the Wolf Creek Community Cemetery at Pine Ridge, South Dakota in 1997. Close by is the now eroded but still fine stone urn marking the grave of muse and socialite **Marchesa Luisa Casati** *(1881-1957)*.

Finally there is **Gus Mears** *(1873-1912)*, the man who founded Chelsea FC in 1904 after Fulham turned down the chance to use the new ground at Stamford Bridge which overlooks this cemetery. Like most of the Magnificent Seven cemeteries, Brompton has its own association dedicated to maintaining community access and conserving nature. The Friends of Brompton Cemetery work tirelessly and no doubt the local foxes, honeybees, moths and butterflies show their appreciation as only they know how.

As an oasis of tranquillity, right in the centre of London, Brompton takes some beating. In recent years the visitor experience has been improved by a new pavillion housing an Information Centre and, opposite that, a smart café located in a Grade II listed building.

Notable Residents:

Squire Bancroft *(1841-1926)* – actor; **Emmeline Pankhurst** *(1858-1928)* – suffragette; **Frederick Leyland** *(1831-92)* – industrialist and art partron; **Richard Tauber** *(1891-1948)* – opera singer; **Samuel Cunard** *(1787-1865)* – ship owner; **Brian Glover** *(1934-97)* – Yorkshire-born actor; **Bernard Levin** *(1928-2004)* – journalist; **Henrietta Moraes** *(1931-99)* – artists' model; **Terence Feely** *(1928-2000)* – screenwriter; **John Snow** *(1813-58)* – pioneer of anaesthetics; **Samuel Sotheby** *(1805-61)* – auctioneer; **John Wisden** *(1826-84)* – founder of the cricket almanac; **Percy Lambert** *(1881-1913)* – motor racing pioneer; **John Jackson** *(1769-1845)* – boxer; **Prince Alexandre Bagration** *(1877-1955)* – Russian prince; **Blanche Roosevelt Macchetta** *(1858-1998)* – opera singer; **Long Wolf** *(1833-92)* – Indian chief; **Marchesa Luisa Casati** *(1881-1957)* – muse and socialite ; **Gus Mears** *(1873-1912)* – founder of Chelsea FC.

Brompton Cemetery

Chiswick New Cemetery (1933)

Staveley Road, W4 2SJ
Tel: 020 8583 6080
Transport: Chiswick Rail; Bus E3, 190
Open: Daily 9am-7pm (Apr-May & Aug-Sep), 9am-8pm (Jun-Jul),
    9am-5.30pm (Mar & Oct), 9am-4pm (Nov-Feb)

Chiswick New Cemetery got under way in 1933 and even now only half of the 15 acre site is in use. One of the earliest residents is William Body, who lies by his son Will who predeceased him in World War I. They rest in a family plot with a dignified memorial inscribed with the words 'In the garden of memory we meet every day'.

There is a large art-deco style chapel capable of seating 80 or more. The brick and stone chapel has weathered very well, its angular lines making it resemble a miniature version of the former power station that is now Tate Modern.

The cemetery grounds have been landscaped like a municipal park and would be a joy if it wasn't for the noise of Chiswick High Road and the trains clattering past, doing their best to ruin the ambience of the scenery.

Interestingly, the cemetery has never actually been consecrated, in order to make interdenominational ceremonies possible. It's also fairly representative of the local Eastern European population, with Russian crosses abounding and the odd Polish grave dotted about here and there.

Chiswick Old Cemetery (1888)

Corney Road, London W4 2RA
Transport: Chiswick Rail; Bus 190, E3
Open: Daily 9am-7pm (Apr-May & Aug-Sep), 9am-8pm (Jun-Jul),
    9am-5.30pm (Mar & Oct), 9am-4pm (Nov-Feb)

Chiswick Old Cemetery was opened in 1888 and is packed solid – it only has space left for family graves. It sits right next to St Nicholas' churchyard, the borders between cemetery and churchyard barely perceptible. As a result, some unusually old graves can be found alongside the relatively recent Victorian ones. None more so than that of **Barbara Villiers, the Duchess of Cleveland** *(1641-1709)*, fabled mistress of 'merry' King Charles II and mother to at least five of his offspring.

Just inside the churchyard's entrance is a large monument bearing a paint palette and an evil-looking mask. This denotes the grand family vault housing the darkly satirical painter and printmaker **William Hogarth** *(1697-1764)*. For an example of good old Victorian splendour, look no further than the family Camar sarcophagus. It is a superb specimen of mid-19th century cemetery ostentation. Another fine example of funeral art is the grand tomb commemorating landscape artist **Philippe de Loutherbourg** *(1740-1812)*, designed by the leading architect of the time Sir John Soane. A more modest grave is that of sculptor **Thomas Thornycroft** *(1815-85)* whose most notable work is the monument to Boadicea outside Parliament.

Other notable residents include American artist **James Abbott McNeill Whistler** *(1834-1903)*, whose Renaissance-style bronze table tomb has suffered from the attentions of local hoodlums who have long since made off with the four corner statuettes, they have since been replaced by fibre-glass replicas. Whistler is now considered to one of the most innovative artists of his generation and has a monument on the north bank of Chelsea Bridge.

Another renowned artist found at Chiswick is **William Blake Richmond** *(1842-1921)*, a Victorian portrait painter whose sitters included Charles Darwin, Otto von Bismarck, and the art and crafts pioneer William Morris. Richmond was also responsible for some of the mosaics in St Paul's Cathedral, and can be located by a sizeable, ornate carving of a woman on his headstone.

It's always humbling to see graves that evoke pivotal events in modern history – none more so than those commemorating victims of disasters. **Arthur Howell Burden** *(1890-1915)* was an Assistant Purser on the transatlantic liner *Lusitania* when it was sunk in 1915 off the coast of Ireland by a German U-boat. His grave can be found under a white cross with a simple circle.

An honourable mention goes to **Frederick Hitch VC** *(1856-1913)*, who won his award for his role in the defence of the famous garrison at Rorke's Drift in 1879 during the Zulu Wars. You'll find him in a granite tomb, draped with a Union Jack and a pith helmet. Talking of renowned British military mishaps, seek out Henry Joy, whose sole claim to fame is that he was the bugler who set in motion the infamous *Charge of the Light Brigade*.

Notable Residents:

Barbara Villiers, the Duchess of Cleveland *(1641-1709)* – mistress of King Charles II; **William Hogarth** *(1697-1764)* – artist; **Philippe de Loutherbourg** *(1740-1812)* – landscape artist; **Thomas Thornycroft** *(1815-85)* – sculptor; **James Abbott McNeill Whistler** *(1834-1903)* – artist; **William Blake Richmond** *(1842-1921)* – artist; **Arthur Howell Burden** *(1890-1915)* – assistant purser on the *Lusitania*; **Frederick Hitch VC** *(1856-1913)* – soldier.

Gunnersbury Cemetery (1929)

143 Gunnersbury Avenue, W3 8LE
Tel: 020 8992 2924
Transport: Acton Town LU, Gunnersbury LU/Rail;
Bus E3 (Acton Town side), H91 (Gunnersbury side)
Open: Daily 9am-8pm (Jun-Aug), 9am-7pm (Apr, May, Sep), 9am-
    5.30pm (Feb, Mar, Oct), 9am-4.30pm (Nov-Jan)

Established in 1929 and situated adjacent to Gunnersbury Park, this unpretentious cemetery is one of the focal points for west London's sizeable Polish community and a must for Polish visitors to London.

Originally part of the Rothschild family's Gunnersbury Park estate, it has aesthetically pleasing, geometric brick chapels and the cemetery as a whole exudes a sense of weather-beaten grandeur. Gunnersbury's entrance drive is lined with displays of flowers and with camellias and roses planted along the side walls. The Garden of Remembrance is a recent addition, which incorporates a smallish section for cremated memorials.

The centrepiece at Gunnersbury is the great black obelisk of the Katyn memorial (dedicated 1976), 'in remembrance of 14,500 Polish prisoners of war who disappeared from camps at Kozielsk, Stavobielsk and Ostaszkow of whom 4,500 were later identified in mass graves at Katyn near Smolensk'. Surrounded (in the summer at least) by ebullient plant life, it stands on the site of what used to be the Roman Catholic chapel until that was bombed in the war. Translated from Polish, the message it conveys is stark: 'The conscience of the world calls for the truth.' The plaque carries an even more brutal statement: 'Murdered by the Soviet secret police on Stalin's orders 1940. As finally admitted in April 1990, by the USSR after 50 years shameful denial of the truth.' The words give some indication of the bitterness that still surrounds the massacre and the struggle to erect this monument in the face of Soviet denial and opposition.

The southern, Roman Catholic, half of the cemetery is dominated by Poles and other eastern Europeans, some clearly with grand origins indeed. There are Christ-like motifs and biblical allusions aplenty, some highly colourful. One man definitely worth seeking out is **General Tadeusz Bor-Komorowski** *(1895-1966)*, the commander of the Polish Resistance during the Second World War and the man who ordered the Warsaw Uprising. The General's grave stone is still at Gunnersbury, but his body was returned to Poland in 1994 where he received a state funeral. Close by is **Prince Vsevolod** *(1914-1973)* of Russia, a cousin of Tsar Nicholas II, the last Russian monarch. Married three times, the Prince's death in 1973 marked the end of the male bloodline of the royal 'Kostantinovich' family.

In the central part of the cemetery is the grave of one of Britain's greatest pianists, **John Ogdon** *(1937-89)*. Ogden came to prominence in 1962 as the joint winner of the Tchaikovsky piano competition. After ten years of success and acclaim he suffered a breakdown and the rest of his life was plagued from what would now be called bipolar disorder. Further along is the simple grave of artist **Sir Matthew Arnold Bracy Smith** *(1879-1959)*, who left a vast body of work to the City of London. **Terrance Donovan** *(1936-96)* was a working class Stepney boy who became one of the most successful photographers of the 1960's and went on to direct over 3,000 TV commercials. His large white stone grave can be found in block D, close to legendary film director **Carol Reed** *(1906-76)* *(Oliver!, The Third Man, Mutiny On The Bounty)* and members of the infamous **Messina** family, a group of Maltese racketeers who thrived in post-war Soho.

Notable Residents:

General Tadeusz Bor-Komorowski *(1895-1966)* – Commander-in-Chief of Polish forces; **Prince Vsevolod** *(1914-1973)* – exiled Romanov; **John Ogdon** *(1937-89)* – painist; **Sir Matthew Arnold Bracy Smith** *(1879-1959)* – painter; **Terence Donovan** *(1936-96)* – photographer and director; **Sir Carol Reed** *(1906-76)* – film director; **Alfred** *(1900-63)* and **Giuseppe** *(1879-1946)* **Messina** – gangsters.

1. William Makepeace Thackeray (1811-63)
2. Richard Parkes Bonington (1802-28)
3. Isambard Kingdom Brunel, (1806-59)
4. William Mulready (1786-1863)
5. Andrew Ducrow (1793-1842)
6. Princess Sophia (1777-1848)
7. Duke of Sussex (1773-1843)
8. Charles Blondin (1824-97)
9. Wilkie Collins (1824-89)
10. Anthony Trollope (1815-82)
11. Charles Babbage (1791-1871)
12. Henry Russell (1812-1900)
13. Terence Rattigan (1911-77)
14. John Diamond (1953-2001)
15. Harold Pinter (1930-2008)

KENSAL
GREEN

LADBROKE GROVE

Chapel

MAIN
ENTRANCE
GATE

HARROW ROAD

GRAND UNION CANAL

Anglican
Chapel

Catacomb

HARROW ROAD

GATE

War
Graves

Crematorium

SCRUBS LANE

Kensal Green Cemetery (1833)

Harrow Road, W10 4RA
Tel: 020 8969 0152
www.kensalgreencemetery.com
   www.kensalgreen.co.uk
Transport: Kensal Green LU & Rail, Ladbroke Grove LU;
Bus 18, 23, 52, 70, 295 & 316
Open: Mon-Sat 9am-6pm, Sun 10am-6pm (Apr-Sep); Mon-Sat
   9am-5pm, Sun 10am-5pm (Oct-Mar)
Tours (approx 2 hours): Every Sunday at 2pm (Mar-Sept), 1st and
   3rd Sunday (Nov-Feb) from the Anglican chapel (see map),
   donation £7 (£5 concessions)

Kensal Green has a special place in the affections of anyone
interested in the history of London's cemeteries. Not only was
it the first commercial London cemetery to be opened, in 1833,
but its vast, gloriously ramshackle fields of eerie catacombs and
Victorian monuments offer an urban treasure hunt that always
throws up something new.

   Kensal Green Cemetery doesn't have quite as many overgrown,
overhanging trees or the lovable mess of Highgate or Abney Park.
Its character is more apparent in its broad, sweeping avenues
which give the endless rows of monuments some space. After
all, the need for a healthy respite from the pollution and crowded
streets of London was part of the rationale behind the creation of
the Magnificent Seven cemeteries in the first place.

   As has been discussed elsewhere, the population explosion of
Victorian London meant that churchyards all over London were
increasingly unable to cope and Kensal Green was chosen as the
site of the first true public cemetery. George Frederick Carden
(1798-1874), the cemetery's founder, had visited Paris in 1821 and
was so struck by the beauty and enormity of the cemetery at Père
Lachaise that he hit upon a scheme to replicate it in London.

   At the main entrance (see map), there is a choice of three roads
leading into the cemetery. The central avenue is the one most
people take, and leads towards the Anglican chapel. Beneath

the chapel lies a catacomb. Originally, coffins were lowered into the subterranean vaults with a mechanical catafalque, which was restored to working order in 1997. As for present-day visitors, they access the vaults via steps within the Anglican chapel.

Kensal Green has an unparalleled mix of architectural styles, with separate chapels for Anglicans and Dissenters and more mausolea than at any other English cemetery. What follows is an edited tour featuring every possible funerary style from Egyptian to Gothic that can be found here.

Novelists, authors and writers are plentiful at Kensal Green, even more so than at Highgate. **William Makepeace Thackeray** *(1811-63)* was a novelist renowned for his clever, satirical works, the finest of which was *Vanity Fair*, a satire on middle class English society. His monument is a stone slab surrounded by railings on the South Avenue beside the Grand Union Canal. Near him can be found landscape painter **Richard Parkes Bonington** *(1802-28)*. Bonington studied in France, and despite his untimely death is widely regarded as one of the great masters of the English School.

A white marble monolith marks the Brunel family plot, on the right as you re-join Centre Avenue. **Isambard Kingdom Brunel** *(1806-59)* is the most famous British engineer of all time, having been responsible for the Great Western Railway, the Clifton Suspension Bridge, and the first transatlantic steamships. His father **Marc Isambard Brunel** *(1769-1849)* was a French immigrant whose greatest achievement was the 18-year project to construct the first tunnel under the Thames. The project won him a knighthood in 1841, but the stress contributed to his death shortly after its completion. Genre painter **William Mulready** *(1786-1863)* has a spectacular tomb, with a recumbent effigy contained within a canopied tomb. At the foot of each of the six columns can be found various instruments of his trade, such as a painter's palette, a rolled-up diploma and a writer's quill.

On the cusp of the inner circle area is the edifice that marks **Andrew Ducrow** *(1793-1842)*, an equestrian trick rider and the kind of flamboyant circus owner that epitomises the

Barnumesque image of Victorian showmen. In death as in life he was centre stage, his Egyptian-style tomb is dedicated to the 'colossus of equestrians' and decorated with beehives, and guarded by two sphinxes either side of the door. It was actually completed five years before his death, at a then princely cost of three thousand pounds.

On your left, is the grand Cooke family monument. A horse stands, bending attentively over a child in a grand scene that looks rather kitsch to modern eyes. Alfred Cooke was a Victorian actor and equestrian (hence the horse) who liked to perform Shakespeare while on horseback.

One of the most breathtaking sights is the monument to **Princess Sophia** *(1777-1848)* on approach to the Anglican chapel. This incredible sarcophagus towers above the visitor with the tomb standing upon a stone plinth. The inscription carries the welcoming message 'Come unto me all that labour and are heavy laden and I will give you rest'. Sophia's own misfortune was to be a daughter of the increasingly eccentric King George III. Poor Sophia was not allowed to marry and was sheltered against her will from outside life. Despite the restrictions Sophia bore an illegitimate child which she was forbidden to keep. Her burial in a public cemetery, helped to give the recently-opened Kensal Green cemetery a greater allure. The aristocracy were initially drawn to Kensal Green after Princess Sophia's brother, **Augustus Frederick, Duke of Sussex** *(1773-1843)*, chose to be buried here (five years prior to Sophia), rather than be deposited like his siblings in the Royal vault at Windsor. Half a century later the grandson of George III, **George William Frederick Charles, second Duke of Cambridge** *(1819-1904)* was buried here in a grand Egyptian-style mausoleum. He is buried alongside the dancer and actress Louisa Fairbrother, who became his wife, much to the dissaproval of the rest of his family.

Leaving the church behind, the next great monument is the twin marble low reliefs of **Charles** *(1824-97)* and **Charlotte Blondin**. Charles, real name Jean-François Gravelet, will always be best known for his amazing feats of tightrope walking, particularly the first crossing of Niagara Falls on a rope in 1859. He went on to cross the falls a further three hundred or so times with increasingly bizarre impediments such as carrying passengers, being blindfolded and even stopping halfway through to cook an omelette.

To the north, **Wilkie Collins** *(1824-89)*, the man responsible for perennial 'A' level set text *The Woman In White*, lies under a simple granite cross. He is buried alongside Caroline Graves, one of his mistresses and the model for *The Woman in White* herself. On one of the paths to the South of the Central Avenue is the plot of novelist **Anthony Trollope** *(1815-82)*. As well as writing some of the greatest novels of the 19th century (*Barchester Towers*, *The Way We Live Now*), Trollope spent many years working for the Post Office, and is credited with having introduced Britain's famous red pillar boxes.

There are inevitably plenty of flowers by the stone that marks the grave of **Steve Ross Porter**, alias **Steve Peregrin Took** *(1949-80)*, Marc Bolan's partner in T Rex. Took died just three years after Bolan's fatal car crash, allegedly choking on a cocktail of chemicals he had bought following the arrival of a long-awaited royalty cheque.

Were it not for **Charles Babbage** *(1791-1871)*, we may not now have the modern world of Social Media and smart phones. A scientist, code-breaker and mathematician, he is commonly regarded as the inventor of the computer. In 1991 a 'difference engine' was completed according to Babbage's original plan and was found to function perfectly. He also developed a mathematical wheel that is a direct ancestor of today's calculator. It is also worth seeking out the lordly stone armchair placed over the grave of prolific Victorian songwriter **Henry Russell** *(1812-1900)*, after his song *The Old Arm-Chair*. He wrote mainly sea songs, the best-known being *A Life On the Ocean Wave*. Nearby is the Rattigan family grave where the ashes of playwright **Terence Rattigan** *(1911-77)* were interred following his death in Bermuda, although his name was never inscribed on the grave. A more

recent arrival is the playwright and diarist **Simon Gray** *(1936-2008)* who wrote over thirty plays and adaptations for the theatre as well as novels and screenplays. A committed smoker, his collected memoirs were entitled *The Smoking Diaries*, the final part of which dealt with his terminal cancer and the experience of living on borrowed time – a theme dealt with by another recent arrival to the cemetery, John Diamond (see below).

The crematorium, designed by G Berkeley Wills, opened in 1939. Along with the typical plethora of wall plaques and flower gardens, one of its features is the mini-cemetery layout of many of the plots with series of headstones clustered close together between pathways, giving the feeling of walking through a Lilliputian cemetery.

In the crematorium, try to find broadcaster **John Diamond** *(1953-2001)*, a brave man who decided to try and cope with throat cancer by writing about it in *The Times* and *Jewish Chronicle*, culminating in a best-selling book *C – Because Cowards Get Cancer Too*. He finally succumbed to the illness in 2001.

A fine ledger stone marks the resting place of playwright, actor and director **Harold Pinter** *(1930-2008)*. Pinter's enigmatic use of silence and vague sense of threat gave rise to the term 'Pinteresque' and his plays acquired international acclaim, culminating in the 2005 Nobel Prize for literature. Another renowned writer and contemporary of Pinter is **James Graham (J.G.) Ballard** *(1930-2009)* who is commemorated with a fine memorial although not buried here.

One man frequently receives visitors even though he isn't in the cemetery. Many a bemulleted European fan has been known to seek out Queen singer **Freddie Mercury**. He was indeed cremated here, but the whereabouts of his ashes are unknown.

Kensal Green Cemetery is Grade I listed on the Register of Parks and Gardens and home to some rare flora and fauna as well as almost a hundred different species of bird. Its sheer size, extending over 77 acres, is one of the reasons it is so special and offers a welcome sanctuary from the busy metropolis.

Notable Residents:

William Makepeace Thackeray *(1811-63)* – author; **Richard Parkes Bonington** *(1802-28)* – landscape painter; **Isambard Kingdom Brunel** *(1806-59)* and **Marc Isambard Brunel** (1769-1849) – engineers; **William Mulready** *(1786-1863)* – painter; **Andrew Ducrow** *(1793-1842)* – circus owner; **Princess Sophia** *(1777-1848)* – daughter of King George III; **Augustus Frederick, Duke of Sussex** *(1773-1843)* – sixth son of George III; **George William Frederick Charles** – second Duke of Cambridge *(1819-1904)* – commander-in-chief of the British army; **Charles Blondin** (aka **Jean-Francois Gravelet**) *(1824-97)* – tightrope-walker; **Wilkie Collins** *(1824-89)* – author; **Anthony Trollope** (1815-82) – novelist.; **Steve Peregrin Took** *(1949-80)* – partner of Marc Bolan in T Rex; **Charles Babbage** *(1791-1871)* – designer of the first computer; **Henry Russell** *(1812-1900)* – songwriter; **Terence Rattigan** *(1911-77)* – playwright; **Simon Gray** (1936-2008) – playwright and diarist; **John Diamond** *(1953-2001)* – writer and broadcaster; **Harold Pinter** *(1930-2008)* – playwright, actor, screenwriter; **James Graham (J.G.) Ballard** *(1930-2009)* – novelist.

Kensington Cemetery (in Hanwell) (1855)

31 Uxbridge Road, W7 3PP
Tel: 020 8992 2924
Transport: Ealing Broadway LU (then bus), Hanwell Rail;
    Bus E8, E11, 83, 207, 607
Open: Mon-Fri 8.30am-6pm, Sat-Sun & Bank Holidays 11am-
    6pm (Mar-Oct); Mon-Fri 11am-6pm, Sat-Sun & Bank Holidays
    11am-4pm (Nov-Feb)

Hanwell has two large cemeteries within its borders, Kensington and Westminster. Both were established in the 1850s when new burial space had to be found within a five-mile radius of the city and the simplest solution was to head west.

Originally a burial ground for the parish of St Mary Abbot, Kensington Cemetery opened in Hanwell in 1855, a year after its neighbour on the south side of the Uxbridge Road, which was aligned to Westminster. By 1924 it was close to capacity and most new interments were transferred to nearby Gunnersbury.

A typically Victorian Gothic archway, designed by Thomas Allom, leads into a picturesque cemetery filled with trees, including holly and yew, which also line the entrance drive. One Gothic style chapel remains complete with stained glass and marble columns, but it is no longer in use and is closed to the public. The paths meander amiably enough around a series of nicely unkempt tombs. Although few tombs stand out, just wander south-west of the chapel to find one – the tall marble cross and statue with a mosaic and lead pavement framed by a set of iron railings, for Mr Wheeler, a local builder.

The memorial to **Edgar Smith** *(1847-1916)*, conchologist (conchology is the study of mollusc shells) at the British Museum, is also worth a peek. His inscription is fast fading but his memorial stone is easily identified by the large, and rather odd, shell-like object on the headstone.

There is also a memorial to the man who locals told me was Hanwell's most celebrated resident, revolutionary psychologist

Dr John Conolly *(1794-1866)*, who in 1839 became superintendent of what was then the Middlesex County Lunatic Asylum but is now St Bernard's Hospital. One of the forefathers of the British Medical Association, Conolly's most notable feat was his pioneering of a 'no-restraint' system of looking after patients as though they were ordinary folk with problems, as opposed to the usually harsh treatment of the mentally ill at the time.

One thing that is striking about Kensington Cemetery is the unusual amount of creepy, ghostly heads impishly poking out of the side of headstones, as if they were caught in the moment of some unfeasibly gruesome demise.

Kensington Cemetery no longer has its own office and all administration of the grounds is based at nearby Gunnersbury Cemetery (see page 103).

Notable Residents:
Edgar Smith *(1847-1916)* – conchologist; **Dr John Conolly** *(1794-1866)* – physician and psychologist.

Margravine Cemetery (1869)

Margravine Road, W6 8RL
Tel: 020 8748 2927
www.margravinecemetery.org.uk
Transport: Barons Court LU; Bus 190, 211, 220, 295
Open: Daily 9am-8pm (May-July), 9am-7pm (Apr & Aug), 9am-
6pm (March & Sept), 9am-5pm (Feb, Oct), 9am-4pm (Nov-Jan)

This is a true greenfield site with over three hundred trees of many different varieties and even two species of bat. It was declared a 'Garden of Rest' in 1951 after almost a century in operation. The old burial ground was established in 1869 and later in 1926 a new cemetery was opened near Kew to serve the area – see Hammersmith New Cemetery (page 133).

You'll more than likely encounter a lot of students walking past hastily when you wander through Margravine Cemetery – it's a popular short cut through the myriad Imperial college campuses.

The octagonal brick Reception House for storing coffins prior to burial is the only building of its kind to survive in its original form in London and was listed Grade II in 2016. One of the most prominent tombs at Margravine has a Corinthian column surmounted by a throne in honour of the Fletcher family, led by patriarch James. This monument is getting a little dirty these days but well represents the way Victorian families saw themselves as mini-dynasties.

Shaded by some imposing trees 'Angels Corner' is a haunting but charming area full of little tombstones marking infants' graves from the 1920s and 1930s. Go there for a sobering glimpse of how widespread infant mortality used to be. Moving on, look for the pillowed bed that contains the wonderfully-named Sexton Cisbert van Os and his wife Adele. Also overlooking the Round Bed is the grave of Susan Marsh and her 9-year-old son Justine George, both of whom lost their lives in the Princess Alice tragedy (see pages 184 and 196). Look out also for Tom Brown, bandmaster, whose grave features a cello propped up against a cross.

South Ealing Cemetery (1861)

South Ealing Road, W5 4RH
Tel: 020 8825 6030
Transport: South Ealing LU;
    Bus 65 from Richmond and Ealing Broadway
Open: Mon-Fri 8am-7.30pm (May-Aug), 8am-7pm (Apr & Sep),
    8am-5.30pm (Mar & Oct), 8am-4.30pm (Nov-Feb),
    open 9am weekends

A clock tower marks the grand entrance to this small but perfectly formed cemetery, surrounded by magnolia trees – in springtime a feast of blossom. Formerly known as Ealing and Old Brentford, the cemetery looks well-maintained and features two chapels in Decorated style. These were built, one for Anglicans, one for Dissenters, and completed by 1873. Since the cemetery's Victorian heyday both chapels have deteriorated and are, at the time of writing, awaiting repair. Recently the roads within the cemetery have been narrowed to make space for new graves, making this very much a working cemetery again.

Like nearby Acton and Gunnersbury, it has a large Polish section, some of whose tombstones are rather more ornate than the usual sober Victorian angels and cherubs. Among the notable names lying here is **Col. Osmond Barnes** *(1834-1930)* who was a distinguished soldier during Victoria's reign. **Frederick Miller** *(1846-1901)* and his wife **Clara Miller** *(1854-1926)* are the parents of author, Agatha Christie. **Spencer H. Walpole** *(1806-98)* is not as well known as his Great Uncle, Prime Minister Robert Walpole, but he did serve as Home Secretary several times under Lord Derby's administration.

Notable Residents:

Col. Osmond Barnes *(1834-1930)* – soldier; **Frederick Miller** *(1846-1901)* & **Clara (née Boehmer) Miller** *(1854-1926)* – Agatha Christie's parents; **Spencer H Walpole** *(1806-98)* – politician.

St Mary's Catholic Cemetery (1858)

679-681 Harrow Road, Kensal Green, NW10 5NU
Tel: 020 8969 1145
Transport: Kensal Green LU & Rail, Ladbroke Grove LU;
Bus 18, 23, 52, 70, 220, 295 & 316
Open: Mon-Sat 8am-5pm, Sun 9am-5pm (Summer); Mon-Sat
     8am-4pm, Sun 9am-4pm (Winter)

Directly adjacent to the magnificent Kensal Green is this fine Roman Catholic cemetery which extends over 29-acres and has become the resting place for over 170,000 Catholic souls since it's opening in 1858. There are several war memorials within the grounds including an impressive Portland stone memorial commemorating the Belgian soldiers killed in World War I. There is also a large Cross of Sacrifice commemorating the British, Irish, French and Canadian servicemen that lost their lives in both World Wars.

At St Mary's you can find the grave of **Gilbert Harding** *(1907-60)*, one of Britain's earliest bona fide TV personalities, a man who became famous for his rudeness on panel shows when the Pop Idol judges were still in nappies. In September 1960 Harding gave a tearful interview to John Freeman revealing the personal unhappiness that lay behind his famously irascible personality. He died just eight weeks later. His grave is an unspectacular flat tomb with a cross. Close to the brown stone mausoleum on the main path is a recently restored marble cross commemorating **Countess Krystyna Skarbek** also known as **Christina Granville** *(1915-52)*, who worked as a spy for British intelligence during the Second World War. She faced many dangers while working for the Special Operations Executive and was awarded a George Medal and the *Croix de Guerre* from the French government. She survived the Gestapo, but died in a Kensington Hotel at the hands of an obsessive man whose advances she had rejected. Close by is the impressive cross marking the resting place of Irish politician and journalist **Thomas Power O'Connor** *(1848-1929)*. O'Connor is little known today, but was a prominent

MP representing Liverpool for many years and one of the most successful journalists and editors on Fleet Street, where his bust still stands. The Barbirolli family have a marble grave that contains the ashes of the famous conductor, **Sir John Barbirolli** *(1899-1970)*. He conducted orchestras around the world but was best known for reviving Manchester's Hallé Orchestra during and after the Second World War. Those familiar with television of the 1970s will recognise the grave and remember the sequinned glamour of **Danny La Rue** (real name Daniel Patrick Carroll) *(1927-2009)* – the most successful drag queen of his generation. Close by is the grave of **Mary Seacole** *(1805-81)* a black nurse from Jamaica who worked to provide care for the wounded soldiers during the Crimean War. Her name was for many years forgotten, but she has now received the recognition she deserves and her grave has been restored and is always adorned with flowers. St Mary's is also the resting place of **George Carmen QC** *(1929-2001)*. He represented Liberal leader Jeremy Thorpe during his trial for conspiracy to murder in 1979 and went on to defend famous names such as Sir Elton John, Imran Khan and Sir Richard Branson. Carmen was renowned for his wit and choleric temper and acquired the nickname 'Killer Carmen'.

St Mary's is not as famous as it's renowned neighbour, but it is a vast cemetery with an impressive list of permanent inhabitants. It is definitely worth visiting in it's own right and is without question the largest and most impressive Catholic cemetery to be found in the Capital.

Notable Residents:
Gilbert Harding *(1907-1960)* – television personality; **Christina Granville** *(1915-52)* – British spy; **Thomas Power O'Connor** *(1848-1929)* – politician and journalist; **Sir John Barbirolli** *(1899-1970)* – conductor; **Danny La Rue** *(1927-2009)* – entertainer; **Mary Seacole** *(1805-81)* – nurse; **George Carmen QC** *(1929-2001)* – barrister.

Westminster Cemetery (in Hanwell)

38 Uxbridge Road, W7 3PP
Tel: 020 8567 0913
www.westminster.gov.uk/hanwell-cemetery
Transport: Ealing Broadway LU (then bus), Hanwell Rail;
  Bus E2, E8, 83, 207, 607
Open: Mon-Fri 8.30am-6pm (Mar-Oct), 8.30am-4.30pm (Nov-
  Feb); Sat-Sun & Bank Holidays 11am-6pm (Mar-Oct), 11am-
  4.30pm (Nov-Feb)

So why is there a Westminster cemetery in the borough of Ealing?
It all boils down to over crowding in Westminster church yards and
the resulting stench.

In the late 1840s St. George's Hanover Square Burial Board
was confronted by complaints about the condition of the burial
grounds in Bayswater Road and St. Mark's, North Audley Street.
They were finally able to take action after the Metropolitan
Interment Act of 1850 became law, and to use modern parlance,
outsourced the new cemetery a few miles west to Hanwell.

It is reputed to have the largest lodge in London, with tall gate
piers that feature a marvelously regal plaque announcing 'City
of Westminster Cemetery'. The chapels were constructed in
the Victorian Gothic style, and feature fine hammer beam roofs
incorporating arched bracing and central carved stone corbels.

At first sight the cemetery looks tremendously opulent, the
gates leading to a row of cedar trees first planted in the 1850s.
Most of the mausolea are nothing too special, apart from the Keller
mausoleum, which is an Egyptian-style pink granite edifice housing
Alexander Keller and family.

One grave here that may be of particular interest to German
visitors, and perhaps to geeky Beatles fans too, is that of English
variety actor **Freddie Frinton**. The man who took his name
from the Essex seaside resort in which he was working (he was
christened Frederick Bittiner Coo), made his name in the 1960s
TV sitcom *Meet The Wife*, which was later namechecked on the
Beatles' legendary *Sgt Pepper* album in 1967. In 1963, he appeared

on German TV as a drunken butler in a sketch named *Dinner For One*, the cult of which endures to this day. It remains a bizarre annual fixture in Germany's New Year's Eve TV schedule. Look out too for the Ottway family plot, topped by a granite tower, and the well-preserved stone for Karen and George Hicks. It dates from 1937, and has a plaque bearing the three lions of England.

Notable Residents:

Freddie Frinton *(1911-68)* – comic actor; **Sir John Hunt** *(1859-1945)* – first town clerk of Westminster; **Richard Newton** *(1854-1926)* – paleontologist.

South-West

Barnes Common Cemetery (1854)

Rocks Lane, SW13 0BY
Transport: Barnes Rail; Bus 33, 72, 265
Open: 24/7 throughout the year

Barnes Common Cemetery could have been so beautiful.
It was the centrepiece of a 1960s plan to create a classic
lawned cemetery in Richmond, but has ended up disused and
overgrown. Nonetheless, meandering through it is a joy for
those plant-loving cemetery aficionados.

For the first century of its life, the cemetery was little more
than an annexe to the local churchyard. Burials went on under
control of the local council and not a lot changed until the
mid-1960s. In 1966 the Borough of Richmond acquired the
cemetery from the church with the intention of turning it into a
lawn cemetery. A lawn cemetery is where, typically, no upright
memorials are allowed but plaques are set in the ground. Initially
the chapel and lodge were demolished and the boundary railings
removed. Unfortunately no further work was undertaken and
over time the cemetery has become overgrown with trees, shrubs
and other plant life.

There are a number of stories about this cemetery dealing with
murder and hauntings, including a story about a ghostly nun who
is said to hover over the cemetery. There have also been various
attempts to clear the paths to make the area suitable for walkers,
but slowly these paths have become overgrown again.

Among the distinguished people that lie buried in the cemetery,
you can find portrait painter **Henry William Pickersgill** *(1782–1875)*,
famous for his seven-decade tenure at the Royal Academy during
which virtually every prominent figure in the country sat for him at
some stage. His wife Jeanette is buried with him – she is said to be
the first person to have been legally cremated in England.

One large monument that still graces the middle of the
cemetery area belongs to the Hedgman family, who were local
Barnes benefactors. It has survived the vandals, time and growth
of the surrounding plants and trees.

Just around the corner, don't forget to seek out one of the most notable landmarks in the area – the tree that killed **Marc Bolan**. There's a constant stream of flowers, notes and messages in honour of the legendary T Rex singer, who was killed at just 29 when his girlfriend's Mini crashed into a tree at Queen's Ride, on Barnes Common in September 1977. In 1997 a memorial was set up beside the tree, and five years later Marc's son Rolan Bolan unveiled a bronze bust at the site to mark the 25th anniversary of the fatal accident. Although the road doesn't actually have a pavement, there's a viewing platform to give fans and visitors the chance to pay their respects. Bolan was cremated and can be found at Golders Green Crematorium.

Notable Residents:
Henry William Pickersgill *(1782–1875)* – artist; **Alexander Finberg** *(1866–1939)* – art historian; **Francis Turner Palgrave** *(1824–97)* – Professor of Poetry at Oxford.

Gap Road Cemetery (1896)

Gap Road, SW19 8JA
Tel: 020 3876 8806
Transport: Wimbledon LU, Haydons Road Rail; Bus 156
Open: Daily 9am-8pm (May-Aug), 9am-7pm (Apr & Sept),
　　9am-5.30pm (Mar & Oct), 9am-3.30pm (Jan-Feb & Nov-Dec)

A measure of how little consideration is generally given to this cemetery is that even Merton Council seems reluctant to give much information except its location. There are two Gothic chapels slap in the centre but they look rather disused. In the south-east corner, an area allocated to Roman Catholics, there is a stone commemorating Belgian refugees from the First World War.

The imposing but faded Cooke mausoleum was once the most impressive sight here and dates from 1885. Its Italianate structure is made of pink and grey granite, with stained glass. Unfortunately it has seen better days and looks like it could do with some maintenance, an observation that sadly applies to much of this cemetery.

Notable names here include Shakespearean scholar **Frederick S. Boas** *(1862-1957)*, who was awarded an OBE in 1953. His first book, *Shakespeare and his Predecessors*, published in 1892, received the following commendation – 'Such a good book, it saves reading Shakespeare.' Something generations of A level students could appreciate.

Also seek out Punch cartoonist **Fred Barnard** *(1846-96)*, best known for his work on Charles Dickens' novels between 1871 and 1879. His death can be attributed to smoking, though it wasn't for the usual reasons – he fell asleep while smoking his pipe and died in the ensuing fire.

Notable Residents:

Frederick S. Boas *(1862-1957)* – Shakespearean scholar; **Frederick Barnard** *(1846-96)* – Punch cartoonist.

Lambeth Cemetery & Crematorium (1854)

Blackshaw Road, SW17 0BY
Tel: 020 7926 4221
Transport: Tooting Broadway LU, Haydons Road Rail;
   Bus 57, 154, 264, 280, 493
Open: Daily 8am-4pm (Nov-Mar), 8am-6pm (April-Oct),
   Sat, Sun and Bank Holidays from 10am

Lambeth is, it's fair to say, not the cemetery it could have been. It was opened in 1854 and was intended to be a classic garden cemetery, but the flat site means that there aren't the climbing paths and misty views of say, Nunhead or Greenwich.

Plaques above the doors of the twin brick Victorian Gothic chapels give a brief history lesson as to the cemetery's early years. The cemetery filled up quickly and pressure on land made the designers plan it on rather utilitarian grounds, with a very geometric arrangement leading to a pattern of square-shaped grave blocks.

There are nonetheless a good few monuments well worth seeking out. Look for the riderless horse standing on top of the plinth for 19th-century equestrian **Thomas Allen**, and a lion resting with intent on a nameless graveside. There aren't really any big names here, but **Charles Chaplin Senior**, music-hall singer and father of his rather more famous namesake son is buried here in an unmarked grave.

The crematorium opened in 1958, and to be frank is much like any other of the time, with a pleasant enough garden of remembrance and a brick chapel.

In nearby Lambeth church, royal fans may want to look out for **Elizabeth Howard**, mother of Henry VIII's wife Anne Boleyn, buried in 'Howard aisle'.

Mortlake Crematorium (1939)

Townmead Road,TW9 4EN
Tel: 020 8876 8056
www.mortlakecrematorium.org
Transport: Kew Gardens LU, Mortlake Rail; Bus 65, 190, 391, R68
Crematorium open: Daily 9am-4.30pm

North Sheen Cemetery (Fulham New) (1926)
& Hammersmith New Cemetery (1926)

North Sheen Cemetery entrance: Lower Richmond Road, TW9 4LL
Hammersmith New Cemetery entrance: Mortlake Road, TW9 4EW
Tel: 020 8878 1934
www.lbhf.gov.uk
Transport: Kew Gardens LU, North Sheen Rail; Bus 65, 190, 391, R68
Cemetery open: Daily 9am-8pm (May-July), 9am-7pm (Apr & Aug),
     9am-6pm (Mar & Sep), 9am-5pm (Feb & Oct), 9am-4pm (Nov-Jan)

Here is the chance to visit two cemeteries and one celebrity-packed crematorium in one go. Both owned by Hammersmith Council despite being in the borough of Richmond, these two 1920s cemeteries run along either side of Mortlake Road (see above for entrance details).

At Hammersmith New, a charming Gothic brick building leads to two chapels that must have been rather opulent looking in their day. There's a central rose garden now past its prime, and the whole place feels somewhat overshadowed by the crematorium that adjoins it.

Mortlake Crematorium is a Grade II listed Art Deco building, built in 1939 to the north side of the cemetery. It won many plaudits upon its opening in 1939, with the man who unveiled it, Lord Horder, the King's physician remarking: 'You seem to have eliminated the sombreness of atmosphere which sometimes shrouds buildings such as these'.

Mortlake is one of the most popular places for the cremation of some of the biggest stars from the UK's post-war entertainment world. Illustrious names to be cremated here include camp icon and *Carry On* star **Charles Hawtrey** *(1914-88)*, Radio 1 DJ and anarchic TV star **Kenny Everett** *(1944-95)*, and comedian and 1970s TV star **Dick Emery** *(1917-83)*. Also here is singer **Kirsty MacColl** *(1959-2000)*, who was tragically killed when struck by a speedboat in Mexico in 2000. She is probably best-known for singing on the Pogues' enduring Christmas hit *Fairytale of New York*, and also had a top 10 hit in 1985 with Billy Bragg's *A New England*. Britain's best loved magician, **Tommy Cooper** *(1921-84)*, was also cremated here. His show was so comically chaotic that when he collapsed on stage the audience took some time to realise it was not part of the act.

These notable names have left their mark on British entertainment, but have left nothing to note their passing at Mortlake. The only exception is the 1970s TV star **Richard Beckinsale** *(1947-79)* who has a plaque noting the passing of one of the great comic actors of his generation. His co-star in *Rising Damp*, **Leonard Rossiter** *(1926-84)* was also cremated here, but again there is no plaque.

North Sheen Cemetery has an impressive entrance gate and brick Gothic chapel which gives onto a flat site organised into a fairly ordinary grid plan. Most of the monuments are marble and few really stand out. The only thing worth taking time out for is the substantial Polish section among the many Roman Catholic graves.

Names cremated here:

Crematorium: **Charles Hawtrey** *(1914-88)* – actor; **Kenny Everett** *(1944-95)* – broadcaster and TV star; **Dick Emery** *(1917-83)* – comedian; **Kirsty MacColl** *(1959-2000)* – singer; **Tommy Cooper** *(1921-84)* – comic magician; **Richard Beckinsale** *(1947-79)* – actor; **Leonard Rossiter** *(1926-84)* – actor.

IN FOND MEMORY OF
BERNARD THOMPSON
WHO DIED 13th. FEB. 1941, AGED 70
AND OF HIS WIFE
ELLEN THOMPSON
WHO DIED 15th MAY 1942, AGED 70.

IN REMEMBRANCE OF
EILEEN MAUD BEDFORD
CALLED TO OUR FATHER
MAY 3rd 1942.
"In His care, our loved one rests".

JOHN ERIC PEARSON
BORN FEB. 18th 1913
DIED APRIL 17th 1942.
Goodnight and God bless you.

IN LOVING MEMORY OF
ARTHUR H. B. GUINNESS
(UNCLE ARTHUR)
DIED 3rd MAY 1944. AGED 58 YRS.
Sadly missed by all.

IN LOVING MEMORY
OF A DEAR MOTHER
ADA SMITH
DIED 16.10.44. AGED 73.

IN LOVING MEMORY OF
MY DEAR HUSBAND

HAROLD BERNARD THOMPSON
"Dear love."
JUNE 26th 1943, AGED 4? YEARS

ELLEN G
BORN 17-8-74. DI
A loving and de

IN LOVING ME
JULIA CHRISTA
DIED 2nd MA
AGED 8

IN LOVING ME
ALBERT W
DIED 4th OC
AGED 7
At Res

IN LOVING ME
HARRIETT
MARCH 29t

IN LOVING MEM
JAMES WILLIAM
DIED 4th MARCH 1942.
ALSO OF ROSA HIS
DIED 6th DECEMBER 19

TO OUR DAR
IN SWEET & PROUD REM
GLADYS
BELOVED DAUGH
JAMES WILLIAM & RO
WHO DIED 18th AUG. 1942.
A loyal wife and lovi

IN EVER LOVING M
JAMES LUDOVIC MAXW

Old Mortlake Cemetery (1887)

Avenue Gardens, SW14 8BP
Tel: 020 8878 1934
Transport: Mortlake Rail; Bus 33, 337, 485, 493
Open: Daily 10am-6.30pm (Apr-Oct), 10am-4.30pm (Nov-Mar)

A small cemetery, Mortlake lies next to Barnes Hospital, between Avenue Gardens and South Worple Way. Its most significant resident is one of the great Victorian social reformers, **Edwin Chadwick** *(1800-1900)*. As Chief Officer of the Poor Law Commission between 1834 and 1854, Chadwick published a damning report on workers' conditions, as well as taking steps to abolish child labour. He also campaigned to stop the use of over-populated churchyards in his *Special Inquiry into the Practice of Interment in Towns* (1843), which nevertheless post-dated the creation of the Magnificent Seven cemeteries in the 1830s and 1840s. He lies beneath a plain grey slab with a fading inscription.

The Dickens family has a significant presence at Mortlake. Charles Dickens is of course elsewhere, in Westminster Abbey, but his editors happened to be his son, known as **Charles Dickens the Younger** *(1837-96)*), and his sister-in-law **Georgina Hogarth** *(1827-1917)*, who are both buried here. Georgina's grassy grave is headed by a cross that reads, at its foot, 'In loving memory of Georgina Hogarth, "Aunty", Sister-In-Law of Charles Dickens'. Despite the failure of Dickens' own marriage, he stayed close to Georgina and referred to her in his will as 'the best and truest friend man ever had'. Charles junior only entered into his father's employ once his own career in business and banking ended in his being declared bankrupt in 1868.

Another significant figure here is **Patrick Hurley**. He was a local Irish Catholic labourer who was murdered in a nearby pub. His burial in the Protestant section at the end of the 19th century prompted a near riot.

Notable Residents:

Edwin Chadwick *(1800-1900)* – Victorian social reformer; **Charles Dickens Jr** *(1837-96)* and **Georgina Hogarth** *(1827-1917)* – editors to Charles Dickens.

Putney Lower Common Cemetery (1858)

Lower Common, Lower Richmond Road, SW15 1JF
Tel: 020 8788 2113
Transport: Barnes Rail, Putney Rail; Bus 22, 33, 72, 265, 485
Open: Mon-Sat 8am-4pm (Nov-Feb), Mon-Sat 8am-5pm (Mar &
Oct), Mon-Sat 8am-6pm (Apr & Sept), 8am-7pm (May-Aug), Sun
opens 10am

Putney Lower Common Cemetery is one of the smallest
cemeteries in London and certainly one of the most rural.
The land originally belonged to Earl Spencer, the Lord of
the Manor, who sold it in 1855. The cemetery opened in
1858, though the burial land was exhausted many years
ago, other than for long-since booked family graves.

Unusually, it blends in seamlessly with the natural open
spaces that surround it, both Putney Lower Common itself and
Barnes Common. Thanks to its mature and natural character, the
cemetery has been designated a site of ecological importance
for the borough of Wandsworth. In the summer the trees
threaten almost to envelop the graves as their greenery stretches
outwards, obscuring the names of long forgotten residents.

The two Gothic entrance gates give way to two run-
down but sturdy old chapels that look like something more
appropriate to a Norfolk village than the busy Thameside.

One mausoleum seems to dominate – a white granite structure
dedicated to a local family of builders, the Avisses, who were
responsible for building the cemetery's ragstone chapels. There
are one or two other interesting tombs, including that of Sir
Alfred Dryden (d.1912), a descendent of John Dryden, the poet.

Putney Vale Cemetery (1891)

Stag Lane, SW15 3DZ
Tel: 020 3959 0090
www.enablelc.org/bereavement
Transport: Putney Rail; Bus 85, 265, K3
Open: Daily 8am-4pm (Jan-Feb & Nov-Dec),
　　8am-5pm (Mar & Oct), 8am-6pm (Apr & Sept),
　　8am-7pm (May-Aug), Sun opens 10am

Putney Vale Cemetery is wonderfully situated, surrounded as it is by Wimbledon Common and Richmond Park, and covers some 47 acres. The Gothic chapel with spire that you encounter at the entrance dates from 1890, and leads to the crematorium established in 1938.

Once inside the cemetery itself, a vast sea of marble, limestone and bronze monuments follows as well as a towering Egyptian mausoleum. The first major sight is the granite cross of the war memorial, leading towards the chapel and the dome with six columns that commemorates local resident Percy Matthew Hart.

An interesting contrast can be drawn between two statues of women close together at the top of the hill. Baroness Frederica Louisa Renwick's sculpture reads 'Love, Service and Sacrifice', while an eerily similar representation of a woman for Lilian Hughes reads 'Love. Life. Happiness.' Two sides of the same coin?

One of the most significant historical sights is the tomb of **Bruce Ismay** *(1862-1937)*. He was the managing director of the White Star Line who owned the ill-fated *Titanic*, and was one of the 700 or so survivors in April 1912. He never lived down his responsibility for the ship's safety and its claim to be 'unsinkable'. Various commissions exonerated him of any guilt, stating that he had actually assisted many passengers in escaping to the lifeboats. His grave is a stone box-like sarcophagus with a low relief carving of three ships in a somewhat choppy sea, and a fitting epitaph, 'They that go down to the sea in ships and occupy their business in great waters, these men see the works of the Lord and His wonders in the deep.'

On the right-hand side, midway through the cemetery, look out for a headstone with two fish and a shell above a heart. 'A joyous man' reads the epitaph for **Roy Plomley** *(1914-85)*, who presented BBC Radio 4's *Desert Island Discs* for over forty years. Plomley created the programme in 1942, in which notable public figures were asked to nominate eight pieces of music, a book, and an inanimate luxury item to take with them for a desert island eternity. You can't help wondering what Roy chose to accompany his final journey...

Across on the left-hand side you can find a man whose role in one of the defining events of the 20th century makes it all the more bizarre that he should have wound up here in south-west London. **Alexander Kerensky** *(1881-1970)* is a name known to all GCSE students as the man who led the Russian Revolution in 1917 – the one that overthrew the Tsar and his family – before he was rather rudely upstaged by Lenin and Trotsky and forced to concede power after just eight months. He was described by Bernard Levin as 'the man who overthrew the Tsars, and was himself overthrown by Lenin'. He fled Russia and lived in New York before being buried here with a monument of a thrice-crossed white cross.

A fascinating oddity is the grave of poor **John Ingram**. Ingram happened to be the resident grave digger at Putney Vale, and according to his modern-looking stone, 'died following an accident in this cemetery, 22 May 1894'. You can be excused for finding a little black humour in that.

Putney Vale's crematorium was probably one of the first in London to attempt to reflect a more ambient, low-key attitude to death, in contrast to the Victorian habit of using the afterlife as an excuse to erect towering edifices. With its brick neo-Georgian styling, rose garden and fountain court, it is arguably the first in a long line of what traditionalists consider to be anodyne and charmless places. I thought it looked lovely and well worth seeing, and the extensive Garden of Remembrance is rather beautiful. Then again I wasn't there in the role of mourner.

A series of plaques around the Garden of Remembrance makes Putney Vale perhaps second only to Golders Green Crematorium for 20th century stars. A treasure trove of TV and movie actors, much-revered historical figures and sports stars have been cremated here, most of whom had their ashes scattered in and around the memorial gardens.

From the world of sport, south-west London's own **James Hunt** *(1947-93)* tops the list. A Wimbledon boy, he epitomised the playboy aspect of Grand Prix like no-one before or since. World Champion in 1976 and hell-raiser extraordinaire, his sudden heart attack in 1993 deprived sport of one of its true characters. Perhaps his spiritual predecessor was **Dick Seaman** *(1913-39)*, a pre-war hero also buried at Putney Vale, albeit whose notoriety mainly comes from the unease generated by his close links to Nazi Germany as Mercedes' number one driver in the 1930s. He died on a Belgian race track before the war started.

Sir Leonard Hutton *(1916-90)* and **Jim Laker** *(1922-86)* were giants from what is usually considered the 'golden age' of English cricket, when players were gentlemen, a firm handshake greeted a wicket and the Barmy Army was unthinkable. Hutton was the first professional, as opposed to 'gentleman', England captain, and for many years his score of 364 runs was a Test match record. Laker's 19 wickets against Australia in Manchester in 1956 is a pretty unbreakable world record, though he may be best-known to many as a TV commentator from the 1970s and 80s.

Those who die young and unfulfilled are always among the saddest of losses, and **Lillian Board** *(1948-70)* is one such. She won gold at the 1969 European Athletics Championships as part of the world record shattering women's 4x400m team, but little more than a year later died from cancer at just 22.

From the acting world, another who died young was **James Beck** *(1929-73)*, Private Walker in BBC TV's *Dad's Army*, who succumbed to a burst pancreas midway through the show's glory years. Also destined to be eternally remembered via endless loops of repeats, are the two female mainstays of the *Carry On* film series, **Hattie Jacques** *(1924-80)* and **Joan Sims** *(1930-2001)*. Scattered here too are the ashes of variety star **Arthur Askey** *(1900-82)*, a music hall veteran and one of Britain's earliest television stars. His career spanned old style music hall right up to appearing as a panelist on the talent show *New Faces* in the 1970s. Finally, a heroine for all generations. There can be no author of children's books more famous than Putney's own **Enid Blyton** *(1898-1968)*, creator of *Noddy* and *The Famous Five* – whose remains were cremated at Golders Green Crematorium but then scattered at Putney Vale.

Notable Residents:
Bruce Ismay *(1862-1937)* – owner of the *Titanic*; **Roy Plomley** *(1914-85)* – radio presenter; **Alexander Kerensky** *(1881-1970)* – revolutionary; **James Hunt** *(1947-93)* – racing driver; **Dick Seaman** *(1913-39)* – racing driver; **Sir Leonard Hutton** *(1916-90)* – cricketer; **Jim Laker** *(1922-86)* – cricketer; **Lillian Board** *(1948-70)* – track athlete; **James Beck** *(1929-73)* – actor; **Hattie Jacques** *(1924-80)* – actress; **Joan Sims** *(1930-2001)* – actress; **Arthur Askey** *(1900-82)* – comedian and actor; **Enid Blyton** *(1898-1968)* – children's author.

Other names to look out for:
Sir Stanley Baker *(1927-86)* – actor and director; **Anthony Blunt** *(1907-83)* – art historian and spy; **Reginald Bosanquet** *(1932-84)* – TV newsreader; **Howard Carter** *(1874-1939)* – Egyptologist and discoverer of Tutankhamun's tomb; **Sandy Denny** *(1947-78)* – folk singer; **David Lean** *(1908-1991)* – film director; **Kenneth More** *(1914-82)* – actor; **Anthony Nolan** *(1971-79)* – boy whose death started the famous bone marrow trust; **Jon Pertwee** *(1919-96)* – actor ; **Donald Pleasance** *(1919-95)* – actor.

St Mary's Cemetery Battersea (1860)

Battersea Rise, Bolingbroke Grove, SW11 1HE
Tel: 020 3959 0090
Transport: Wandsworth Town Rail; Bus 77, 219
Open: Daily 8am-4pm (Jan-Feb & Nov-Dec), 8am-5pm (Mar & Oct),
   8am-6pm (Apr & Sept), 8am-7pm (May-Aug), Sun opens 10am

St Mary's is an L-shaped cemetery, laid out on a grid pattern. Despite being in what looks like a heavily residential part of Clapham, it is actually within a conservation area and is a decidedly pleasant place to be, especially in summer when the mature trees are in full leaf.

There are two small stone Gothic chapels, though only one remains in use. The cemetery retains its original cast iron entrance gates decorated with religious motifs and brick gate piers. Once in, like many cemeteries of its type, the most impressive monuments are close at hand. A monolith commemorates **John Burns** *(1853-1943)*, local Liberal MP from 1894-1912, and the man responsible for building the area's Latchmere Estate. One of the classic Westminster social engineers of his time, Burns was, according to the inscription on his tombstone 'A brave man, an honest politician and a kindly neighbour. He has left behind him a fragrant memory and a good example.'

One of the best sights is the large flaming urn, resembling a very large boiled egg, that signals the memorial for Kaikhoshru Puntheki, a Parsee lawyer from Bombay. Otherwise, the scenery is relatively ordinary, the monotony broken by the abundance of rhyming inscriptions that pervade here. These range from the pitiful to the pithy, and are well worth seeking out and comparing.

For grief-stricken romanticism, look for Alfred Fell and Arthur Ronald, the two boys who drowned age 19 in 1873, and who were mourned with the following ditty: *'Mark the brief story of a summer's day; at noon, in youth and health they launched away Ere eve, death wrecked the bark and quenched the light; the parents' home was desolate at night.'*

Conversely, John Goodman's tomb of 1916 betrays a certain desire to get off the world's irksome axis: *'Farewell, vain world; I've had enough of thee, And now am careless what thou say'st to me.'*

Cemeteries such as St Mary's often reveal how the people who lived near major transport hubs were at risk, and a number of tombs carry inscriptions relating to railway deaths at nearby Clapham Junction station.

One such victim, Henry Blunden, died in 1871 aged just 22 and the local poets had this to say about him: *'All you that come my grave to see, oh think of death and remember me, Just in my prime and fully skilled, when on the railway I was killed.'* Also here is Henry Meyer, the ornithologist whose *Illustrations of British Birds* was published in 1841, and William Bishop, a medical historian who founded the Wellcome Historical Medical Library in 1949.

St Mary Magdalen's, Mortlake (1852)

61 North Worple Way, SW14 8PR
Tel: 020 8876 1326
www.stmarymags.org.uk
Transport: Mortlake Rail; Bus 3, 209, 337, 41933
Open: Daily 9am-3pm

Pre-Magnificent Seven era churchyards are not really the main theme of this book, but the cemetery at St Mary Magdalen's Catholic Church has begun to receive a superb makeover in recent years, and this combined with its historical heritage makes it well worth a visit.

Until recently, those who wandered into the jungle-like park were faced with towering weeds and neglected graves, which was not really surprising as burials stopped here over 30 years ago. Most of the graves had become barely visible thanks to a combination of natural damage, neglect and vegetation, but community work has done much to restore their glory.

The feeling of a wilderness is still present, but the tree stems are now clear of fusty, unnecessary shrubbery, opening the way for some outstanding finds. The biggest attraction here is undoubtedly the tomb of the famous explorer and linguist, **Sir Richard Burton** *(1821-90)*, whose body lies in a stone replica of an Arab tent. Burton travelled extensively in north-east Africa, and visited holy cities such as Mecca, Medina and the forbidden city of Harer disguised as an Arab pilgrim so as to avoid the possibility of execution. He and his colleague and rival John Speke later became the first Europeans to see Lakes Tanganyika and Victoria.

Sitting incongruously in front of an unprepossessing 1920s semi-detached house, Burton's imposing 'tent' is an impressive sight. Its sides were sculpted to create the illusion of the canvas being tugged by a desert wind. It certainly looks like such an animate object until you get up close. The door may feature a crucified Christ figure, but inside, the roof is decorated with a frieze of Islamic stars and crescents.

The two coffins inside can be seen through a plate glass window at the rear of the tomb. If you look really carefully you may be able to see photographs of Burton and his wife Isabel, the other coffin's occupant.

Near Burton is **John Francis Bentley** *(1839-1902)*, best known for being the architect responsible for Westminster Cathedral. His tombstone, simple but elegant, was designed by John Marshall, his loyal assistant, who succeeded him as Cathedral Architect.

This is one of the cemeteries to visit if you want to find assorted admirals, colonels, barons, knights and high-powered people in general. Among the hundreds of graves is the strangely symmetrical Prince of Paris mausoleum which houses the bodies of a seven-year-old French count (pretender to the French throne) and his mother. The Mausoleum was even equipped with real clothes, toys and household equipment such as brushes and dusters that the young count's servants would have used, and which can still be seen to this day.

Notable Residents:
Richard Burton *(1821-90)* – explorer; **John Francis Bentley** *(1839-1902)* – architect.

Streatham Park Cemetery (1909)

Rowan Road, Streatham Vale, SW16 5JG
Tel: 020 8679 4164
Transport: Streatham Common and Mitcham Eastfields Rail;
Bus 60, 118, 152, 463
Open: Daily 8am-4pm (Nov-Mar), 8am-5pm (April-Oct)

Streatham Park began life as the Great Southern Cemetery in 1909 with a post-Victorian brief to eschew wild landscaping and to prioritise making itself the principal final resting place for south Londoners. During its first three decades Streatham Park accounted for about 20% of all burials in south London, according to Hugh Meller in his book *London Cemeteries*.

The cemetery is a fairly haphazard mix of the kind of Gothic style monuments you'll find in a country churchyard, and clean, modernist gardens and polished marble mausolea – the most recent of which was established in 1998. There are a pair of interesting Gothic chapels, but they look somewhat time worn.

Its crematorium (now known as the South London) was opened in 1936 and features a chapel, a columbarium and an anodyne Chapel of Remembrance which serves its function without meriting much of a visit. Beyond that, the memorial gardens look pretty, but resemble a cross between the *Blue Peter* garden and a suburban attempt at a TV-style garden makeover.

A large stone plaque features over 200 names from the 'golden age' of variety, music hall and light entertainment between the wars. Its roll-call of names looks like a bizarre, faded war memorial. Perhaps the most enduring name to be found here is legendary comic actor **Will Hay** *(1888-1949)*. Hay is best-known as the star of the kind of daft but harmlessly comic film associated with the 1930s and early 1940s, such as *Where There's a Will* (1936) and *Oh, Mr Porter!* (1937). Less well-known is that he was multi-lingual, was King of the exclusive showbusiness 'club' the Grand Order of Water Rats, and also happened to be an astronomer – it was he who first discovered a white spot on the planet Saturn in 1933.

The Variety Artists section has a vast, lonely, battered-looking memorial featuring five columns of names – a roll-call of artists buried there in mainly unmarked graves. One such grave houses actress **Connie Smith** *(1875-1970)*. She was an American music hall and variety star who went on to become one of Britain's most respected black actresses. She was born in Brooklyn in 1875, but came to London when she was 21. She made her West End debut in *Showboat* alongside Paul Robeson and continued performing past her 90th birthday.

Star of the 1960s easy listening era, **Dorothy Squires** *(1915-1998)* was born in Wales and was married to James Bond star Roger Moore for 16 years. She can be found in a family plot, with a horizontal stone at ground level – it reads 'With all my heart, I love you'. She was in residence at a north London club when the Krays (see Chingford Mount Cemetery on page 188) caught up with Jack 'the Hat' McVitie and 'sorted him out'.

There are a couple of intriguing grave stones to see if you look around the sparser areas of the cemetery. A shiny granite headstone marks Victoria Cross recipient **Arthur Cross** *(1884-1965)*, whose citation states that the medal was awarded for 'extreme gallantry and supreme devotion to duty' in 1918 after Cross forced seven German soldiers to surrender and hand over their machine guns, armed only with a revolver. Another fascinating, typically pre-war gravestone commemorates Maurice Selbach (1889-1935), killed while cycling. His headstone tells us that 'He died as he had lived, a cyclist', and further evidence of this comes from the slightly bent cycle etched on the stone, with a wheel carved at the top where a cross would normally be found.

Notable Residents:
Will Hay *(1888-1949)* – comedian and actor; **Connie Smith** *(1875-1970)* – actress; **Dorothy Squires** *(1915-1998)* – singer; **Arthur Cross** *(1884-1965)* – soldier.

Wandsworth Cemetery (1878)

Magdalen Road, SW18 3NP
Tel: 020 3959 0090
Transport: Wandsworth Common Rail; Bus 77, 219
Open: Mon-Sat 8am-4pm (Jan-Feb & Nov-Dec), 8am-5pm (Mar &
   Oct), 8am-6pm (Apr & Sept), 8am-7pm (May-Aug),
   Sun opens 10am

Wandsworth Cemetery is a large, wedge-shaped cemetery dating
from 1878. The sloping main drive along Magdalen Road looks
out over the Wandle Valley and into the green of Surrey.

The two Gothic chapels were damaged by bombs during the
Second World War, one of the chapels has part of its façade
missing and is out of use. These lead into a pleasant but ultimately
quite plain cemetery, with still present reminders of the war
damage the area suffered. Many of the older monuments can be
found at the various crossroads where the grid style paths meet.
Solid plinths topped by urns, obelisks and crosses are plentiful.
The cemetery is home to an impressive eight war memorials, set
in formal planting, and the remains of no less than two air raid
shelters. The area is scattered with monuments to the fallen from
the First World War.

Look out for Ness Wilson, whose tombstone message is
as long as a thank you speech at the Oscars. Wilson's 'life of
unwearied effort in permanently improving the condition of the
poor and needy' evidently made him one of Victorian London's
unsung heroes.

South-East

Brockley & Ladywell Cemeteries (1858)

Brockley Road, SE4 2QY & Ladywell Road, SE13 7HY
www.foblc.org.uk
Tel: 020 8314 3210 / 9635
Transport: Crofton Park, Ladywell and Brockley Rail;
    Bus 122, 171, 172, P4
Open: Daily 10am-5pm (Mar-Oct), 10am-4pm (Nov-Feb)

Up to the amalgamation of the London boroughs of Deptford
and Lewisham in 1965, the current Brockley Cemetery was the
Deptford Cemetery, and Ladywell Cemetery was Lewisham
Cemetery. A grassy ridge now marks the former dividing wall.
Ladywell's Dissenters' chapel is the only surviving chapel and,
following renovation in 2004, is still in use today.

Decorative iron gates still marked 'Ladywell Cemetery' lead into
a series of meandering pathways, then towards large granite tombs
in an L-shaped avenue. Many of the monuments in the Brockley
Cemetery are to sailors and other characters from the maritime
world – a reminder of Deptford's rich dockland past.

There are several notable people buried in the two cemeteries.
Buried in Ladywell is **Ernest Dowson** *(1867-1900)*. One of the
'decadent' poets of the 1890s, he was an alcoholic son of two
suicides and died of tuberculosis, penniless. Dowson's aphorisms
are his enduring legacy, many such as 'They are not long, the days
of wine and roses' and 'Gone with the wind', have entered popular
usage. His grave, in the Ladywell Roman Catholic section, was
restored by public subscription and a service held in August 2010
after completion. It is well worth a visit whether or not you have a
penchant for Wildean quips.

In the Ladywell side of the cemetery, look out for a high column
with a stone effigy of a young child looking to the heavens. This
marks the resting place **Jane Maria Clouson** *(1854-71)*. The
inscription relates that she was 'a motherless girl who was
murdered in Kidbrooke Lane on Tuesday the 25th of April 1871'.
Jane died five days later under the care of Guy's Hospital. She
must have made an impression on those who tried to help her

as the inscription reads, 'She was agreeable in manner, amiable and affectionate in disposition'. Her last words are recorded for perpetuity 'Oh let me die'. This grand column was erected by public subscription and stands alone in its own small section of the cemetery.

Brockley and Ladywell cemetery is a place of contrasts. The central area contains some of the oldest graves such as that of Henry Brooke who 'departed this life' aged just 42 and whose ivy covered grave stone was erected in 1862, just four years after the opening of the cemetery. These neglected graves have been left to form an unkempt nature reserve, while the periphery of the cemetery grounds are still accepting new arrivals. Towards the Ladywell entrance lies **Mary Elizabeth Macrae** *(1942-2009)*, a local poet who published two books of poetry. Just behind Macrae's simple stone is the grave of Julia Nunn, who is described in very simple terms as 'Academic & Hedonist'. A sentiment that would make some of the Victorian inhabitants of the cemetery shudder with disapproval.

A new nature trail has been created as part of the renovations at the cemetery, and a meadowland bustling with purposeful activity give the cemetery the feeling of a living, breathing place.

Notable Residents:

Ernest Dowson *(1867-1900)* – poet; **Jane Maria Clouson** *(1854-71)* – murder victim; **Mary Elizabeth Macrae** *(1942-2009)* – poet.

Camberwell New Cemetery (1927)

Brockley Gardens, Forest Hill, SE23 3RD
Tel: 020 7525 5600
Transport: Honor Oak Park Rail;
    Bus P2, P3, P4, P12, 63, 484
Open: Daily 8.30am-7pm (Apr-Sept), 8.30am-5pm (Oct-Mar),
    Sun opens 10am

Camberwell New Cemetery was opened in 1927 in order to provide more space, because Camberwell Old Cemetery was full. Its two stately chapels divided by an imposing central tower were designed by Sir Aston Webb and are an impressive sight. Camberwell New is also home to Honor Oak Crematorium, whose stained glass windows were designed in 1939 by Webb's son Maurice. The crematorium's Italianate style was intended to resemble the campanile of the cathedral in Venice.

There aren't many outstanding monuments here, but look out for the boxer figure and car that commemorates former world light-heavyweight champion **Freddie Mills** *(1919-65)*, whose death was for many years considered suicide, but is now thought to have been murder at the hands of criminal associates. Close by is another hard man, **William Pullum** *(1887-1960)*. Pullum was a 9 stone weakling who took up weightlifting in 1905 and in the course of the next 15 years broke 192 world records. He was, according to his headstone, 'a pillar of strength'. Another key figure in modern East End folklore is buried here. **George Cornell** *(d.1966)* was the man who was famously shot by Ronnie Kray in the 'Blind Beggar' pub. Apparently Cornell calling Kray 'a fat poofter' was too much for Ron's volatile temper. Camberwell New Cemetery is still very much in use and in recent years has expanded southward into surrounding public land to accommodate the new arrivals.

Notable Residents:

Freddie Mills *(1919-65)* – boxer; **William Pullum** *(1887-1960)* – weightlifter; **George Cornell** *(d.1966)* – East End gangster.

Camberwell Old Cemetery (1856)

Underhill Road, SE23 0RU
Tel: 020 7525 5600
Transport: Honor Oak Park Rail;
    Bus P4, P12, 63, 122, 171, 172;
Open: Daily 8am-7pm (Apr-Sept), 8am-5pm (Oct-Mar),
    Sun opens 10am

One of London's pleasantly derelict cemeteries, Camberwell Old Cemetery has seen better days but still retains a certain charm.

Along with several other parishes bordering London, the 1850s found Camberwell in dire need of extra burial space. The Camberwell Burial Board was set up to find a solution to the problem, taking its cue no doubt from the instant success of nearby Nunhead. As a result, in 1855 the board bought 30 acres of meadowland and established the Burial Ground of St Giles, Camberwell which is now known as Camberwell Old Cemetery. The first burial took place in July 1856 and by 1874 the cemetery had 30,00 permanent residents requiring the purchase in that year of a further 7 acres of neighbouring farmland to meet the growing demand.

The Gothic lodge and chapels were designed by George Gilbert Scott, the surveyor of Westminster Abbey and the architect of the still dazzling St Pancras station, and the Albert Memorial. Unfortunately not much of Scott's work remains here, just the lodge which is now a private residence. The three chapels, one for Anglicans, one for Catholics and one for Nonconformists, finally bit the dust and joined the cemetery's permanent residents in the 1970s. The collection of war memorials in the north-east corner are testament to the damage inflicted on the area by Zeppelins during the First World War.

Notable Residents:

Frederick J. Horniman *(1835-1906)* – Tea merchant, traveller, collector and founder of the Horniman Museum.

Charlton Cemetery (1855)

Cemetery Lane, SE7 8DZ
Tel: 020 8856 0100
Transport: Charlton Rail, Woolwich Dockyard Rail;
   Bus 53, 54, 422, 486
Open: Daily 9am-7pm (Apr-Sept), 9am-4pm (Oct-Mar)

The cemetery was founded in 1855 as a 'Gentleman's Cemetery' on land which was originally part of the estate of Sir Thomas Wilson. Other than the addition of seven acres, it has barely changed since the publication of a drawing in the *Illustrated London News* in 1857 showing its Victorian layout. The two 19th-century chapels are in contrasting styles. The Church of England chapel is in Early English style with stained glass windows, while the now disused Roman Catholic Chapel is in Decorated style. The cemetery retains its original stone-capped walls topped with railings and a restored, tile-hung lodge.

One of the more unusual sights here is the tomb of Jemima Ayloy. A young local girl, her death in 1860 was marked by a medieval-style effigy beneath a dome-shaped canopy. It is said that the vault that holds her mortal remains is a whopping 22 feet deep, and to this day houses tables and chairs so that relatives could (or indeed, still can) pay their respects.

Unsurprisingly for such a dockside location, there are numerous monuments to those who fell in the process of building Britian's empire. Walk around for a while and lose count of the victims to drowning, scurvy and fever, war wounds and so on. Not least the 52 who died of yellow fever on *HMS Firebrand* in July 1861, commemorated by an urn on a large plinth.

Among the monuments to the army and navy and personnel connected with the Royal Artillery at Woolwich, is the monument to **Admiral Sir Watkin Pell** *(1788-1869)*, a man who served with Lord Nelson and who likewise lacked a major limb. Pell lost his leg when just a young midshipman, but rose to be knighted in 1837, having 'got so accustomed to the ways of a cork leg'.

In fact, walking around Charlton is like a concise lesson in England's military and naval history. **Admiral George Perceval** *(1794-1874)*, 6th Earl of Egmont was a midshipman at the Battle of Trafalgar in 1805; **Sir William Dalyell** *(1784-1865)* fought in the Napoleonic wars, and Charlton is also the resting place for various Governors of Malta, Bermuda, Gibraltar, and the commander-in-chief of India. **Sir Geoffrey Callender** *(1875-1946)*, the first Director of the National Maritime Museum is also buried here.

On a completely different note, the memorial of **Thomas Murphy** (d.1932), owner of Charlton greyhound track, features a pair of greyhounds at the foot of Corinthian columns.

Unfortunately, vandalism has been a regular problem at Charlton. On one night in March 2004, 49 headstones were knocked over, broken and headstone photos removed. Most of the damage has been repaired but some signs of the vandalism are still evident today.

Notable Residents:
Admiral Sir Watkin Pell *(1788-1869)* – naval hero; **Admiral George Perceval** *(1794-1874)* – naval hero; **Sir William Dalyell** *(1784-1865)* – naval hero; **Sir Geoffrey Callender** (1875-1946) – Director of the National Maritime Museum; **Thomas Murphy** (d.1932) – dog track owner.

Eltham Cemetery & Crematorium (1935)

Crown Woods Way, SE9 2RF
Tel: 020 8856 0100
Transport: Falconwood Rail; Bus B15, B16
Open: Daily 9am-7pm (Apr-Sept), 9am-4pm (Oct-Mar)

Eltham Cemetery, also known as Falconwood, is one of London's flattest cemeteries, especially compared with the rolling hills of Greenwich. Given the terrain, it's not surprisingly based on a grid pattern, with trees only along the paths and edges. The Gothic brick chapels are fairly standard for the time, tidy, unfussy and bereft of any architectural frills.

There are some worthwhile sights, such as a half-size figure of a man dressed in flying gear commemorating an airman killed in 1938. It's not easy to miss – his outfit looks more like a post-apocalyptic anti-radioactivity suit than anything else.

One grave to seek out is that of **Richmal Crompton** *(1890-1969)*, the woman responsible for penning dozens of *Just William* books and short stories between 1922 and 1969, and giving birth to the immortal Violet Elizabeth character. Crompton attempted to write books for adults but these were never as successful.

The adjoining crematorium dates from 1956. The chapel is said to resemble a scaled down version of Liverpool's Roman Catholic cathedral. The flower bed and rose garden are typical of a crematorium – nothing out of the ordinary or wildly exciting, but pretty all the same.

Notable Residents:

Richmal Crompton *(1890-1969)* – author.

Greenwich Cemetery (1856)

Well Hall Road, Eltham, SE9 6UA
Tel: 020 8856 0100
Transport: Eltham Rail; Bus 89, 122, 161, 244, 286
Open: Daily 9am-7pm (Apr-Sept), 9am-4pm (Oct-Mar)

The panoramic views from the top of the hill are the most impressive aspect of Greenwich Cemetery. Few others can offer such a vast panorama of London, not even Highgate. The aim here, like many other ambitious Victorian cemetery projects, seems to have been to rival the views of Paris seen from Montmartre cemetery.

The main path leads neatly up to the two large Gothic chapels that stand atop the hill, with a lodge dating from the 1930s. Around the cemetery are grand railings interspersed by solid brick piers with stone capitals.

With the military academy and Woolwich Arsenal nearby, many soldiers are buried here. The 'Great War Heroes Corner' has the best views towards Crystal Palace and the city, and the Commonwealth Burial Ground is a compact but well-tended area. There is also a special Norwegian section for refugees of the Second World War, and a children's section easily identified by the large amount of heartbreakingly small headstones.

It's also worth trying to find the memorial to Russian dissident writer **Nicholas Ogareff** *(1814-1877)*. He lived in exile in Greenwich until his death in 1877, but was exhumed 89 years later in 1966 when the Cold War had thawed enough to enable his body to be sent back to Moscow for burial in a columbarium at the Kremlin.

Overall, the view may be great, but most of the monuments are rather plain in comparison. However, you can still find several unusual coffin-shaped headstones, rarely seen in London.

Grove Park Cemetery (1935)
Marvels Lane, SE12 9PU
Tel: 020 8314 3210
Transport: Grove Park Rail; Bus 124, 126, 273, 284
Open: Daily 10am-5pm (Mar-Oct), 10am-4pm (Nov-Feb)

Another hilltop cemetery, Grove Park lies in the extreme south-east corner of Lewisham borough, bordering a pleasant semi-rural area of neighbouring Bromley, known as Chinbrook Meadows. The surrounding woodland has helped shape the cemetery grounds with mature alder, oak, beech, hornbeam, hazel and pine lining the paths and helping to subdivide this deceptively large, rolling landscape.

The cemetery chapel is large but dilapidated, resembling a neglected cricket pavilion, but the grounds are well maintained with on-going work to keep the vegetation at bay and prepare new plots. The more recent graves are often marked by photos, handwritten notes and fresh tokens of loss.

The people buried here are as diverse as the plant life with the West Indian, Chinese, Greek, Thai and Italian communities all represented and one area dedicated to London's Turkish community. Grove Park was established in 1935 and so there are none of the grand Victorian graves to be found at nearby Nunhead or West Norwood cemeteries, with just a handful of angel figures to be found on the entire site. This lack of grand monuments has not limited expressions of grief, with heartfelt engraved messages, a weathered football boot laying on one young footballer's grave and another showing the departed in his racing prime on a speeding motorbike. There is even a sculpture of a sports car, marking the resting place of one young car fanatic. The more sober graves of fallen soldiers are distributed throughout the cemetery, but towards the far end there is a large screen listing the names of local residents who died in the Second World War with numbered stone markers showing their exact place of rest.

Grove Park may be little known, but it does possess some charm and is definitely a pleasant place to explore if you find yourself in this suburban part of south-east London.

Hither Green Cemetery (Lee) (1873)

Verdant Lane, SE6 1JX
Tel: 020 8314 3210
Transport: Hither Green Rail, Grove Park Rail; Bus 124, 284
Open: Daily 10am-5pm (Mar-Oct), 10am-4pm (Nov-Feb)

Hither Green Cemetery was founded in 1873, and sprawls merrily along the side of Verdant Lane. Originally known as Lee Cemetery, its well-tended, meandering grounds and smart Gothic chapel give it a tranquil atmosphere, with gargoyles and spires aplenty. Adding to the ambience is a pleasant sense of disarray given by the tombstones that sit up in angular rows, like a rather haphazard army.

While it is by no means as wild as some cemeteries in this book, Hither Green is undoubtedly a magnet for animal life. Native woodland birds certainly seem to like it as well as, a bizarre addition to south London life, ring-necked parakeets who feed and roost in the area. The nature angle doesn't end with the cemetery itself. On the eastern edge of the cemetery Hither Green Nature Reserve is a haven for a diversity of wild plants and animals.

The most significant memorial at the cemetery is that which recalls the bombing of the nearby Sandhurst Road School in 1943, in which 38 children and 6 members of staff were killed. The mass grave for victims of that awful event, still brings a lump to the throat. In the far corner you can find 'Railway Children Walk', commemorating author **Edith Nesbit** *(1858-1924)*, who lived in nearby Baring Road. She was a founding member of the Fabian Society in the 1890s, and was well-known for the charity work she did among the poor of Deptford. The cemetery's architect **Francis Thorne** is close by, buried here in 1885.

The red brick crematorium, sometimes referred to as Lewisham Crematorium, was built in 1956. It has a pond, small stream and labyrinthine paths – offering some tranquility for visiting mourners.

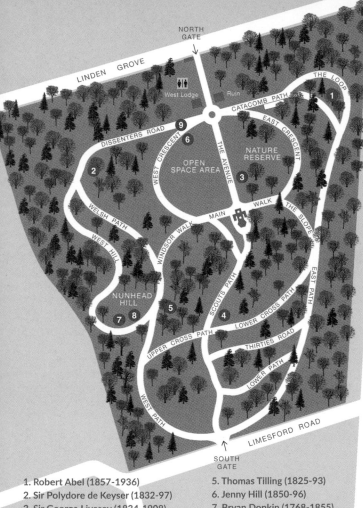

1. Robert Abel (1857-1936)
2. Sir Polydore de Keyser (1832-97)
3. Sir George Livesey (1834-1908)
4. Jem Ward (1800-84)
5. Thomas Tilling (1825-93)
6. Jenny Hill (1850-96)
7. Bryan Donkin (1768-1855)
8. John Allen (1790-1865)
9. Scottish Martyrs Memorial

Nunhead Cemetery (1840)

Linden Grove, SE15 3LP
Tel: 020 7525 5600
www.fonc.org.uk
Transport: Nunhead Rail; Bus 78, 343, 484, P12
Open: Daily 8am-7pm (Apr-Sept), 8am-5pm (Oct & Mar),
8am-4pm (Nov-Feb)
Conducted general tours last Sunday of every month at
2.15pm, other tours listed on website. Meet at Linden
Grove gates

Nunhead Cemetery is not usually the first of London's Victorian cemeteries to spring to mind, but south Londoners hold it as dear as most north Londoners do Highgate, and it is arguably the most attractive of all. It's also second only to Kensal Green in size, and has a wonderfully tranquil feel throughout its 52 acres of elegant wilderness. Much of it remains overgrown and creepy, but that is undeniably one of its attractions.

The imposing entrance gates, flanked by two Lodges, and formal avenue make for a stately welcome, but the towering limes of the main drag soon clear to reveal open, meandering country-like paths that you don't get elsewhere in and around Peckham. The octagonal ruined Anglican chapel is at the crest of the hill and was designed by the once popular architect Thomas Little. It is in Gothic revival style and overlooks a large, shady woodland area. Nunhead has benefited from the programme of gentle restoration begun in 1981 when the 'Friends of Nunhead Cemetery' was formed.

Restoration was needed here more than at any other Magnificent Seven cemetery. A gradual decline in maintenance by the owners from the war years onwards reached its nadir in 1969 with the cemetery's closure. Nunhead changed ownership when the local borough stepped in to buy the cemetery for a nominal £1 in 1975 and set about converting the unruly wasteland into a modern lawn cemetery. Opposition to this approach from local residents led to the formation of the Friends of Nunhead Cemetery.

In 1999-2000 an extensive restoration project was funded by Southwark Council and the Heritage Lottery Fund. A total of 55 memorials were restored, railings replaced and paths resurfaced along with stabilising the magnificent ruined Anglican chapel and its crypts. Some purists mourn the transformation of part of the original wild Victorian necropolis into what they consider to be little more than a glorified park. But the transformed Nunhead, with its combination of undulating shrub-lined pathways and a nature reserve, has many devotees. It is also one of the best bird nesting sanctuaries in London.

Nunhead is not really the first place to go if you're star-spotting, but there are hundreds of headstones that hint at all manner of fascinating stories, peopled by the most incredible characters recalled in the Friends four volumes of Nunhead Notables. There's a Scottish African explorer, two residents who fought in the American Civil War, an Irish freethinker, a French Huguenot marquis, eight veterans of the Waterloo campaign and three dashing cavalrymen who survived the Charge of the Light Brigade. England test cricketer **Robert Abel** *(1857-1936)*, who held the record for highest score made at the Oval for many years, also lies here. Nunhead is also the place of rest for many music hall stars such as **Jenny Hill** *(1850-96)* whose vibrant performance earned her the nickname 'The Vital Spark'. **Jem Ward** *(1800-84)* was one of the country's great bare-knuckle fighters who became champion despite having been the first fighter to be censured for deliberately losing a fight. Following his retirement, Ward became a successful painter. The engineer and inventor **Bryan Donkin** *(1768-1855)* has a large family vault in Nunhead. Donkin worked with the Brunel's on the Thames Tunnel and constructed the world's first computer in the form of Babbage's difference engine, he also patented the first metal tin to store food. Look out for an unusual headstone bearing two theatrical masks in memory of actor Calvin Simpson, and a monument commemorating the 'Leysdown Tragedy' of 4 August 1912, when nine scouts were drowned off the coast at Leysdown,

Isle of Sheppey. One victim, William Beckham is related to former England football captain, David Beckham.

Also worth searching out is the obelisk dedicated to five 18th-century Scottish political agitators whose radical demands for parliamentary reform led them to be transported to Australia in 1793 – they became known as the 'Scottish Martyrs'.

In among the wartime and industrial-age disasters there is occasionally a sobering reminder of the dangers of the modern world – witness the stone commemorating six members of the Oxlade family who died in an air crash in Perpignan, France in 1963.

Notable Residents:
Robert Abel *(1857-1936)* – Test cricketer, **Jenny Hill** *(1850-96)* – music-hall artiste; **Jem Ward** *(1800-84)* – bareknuckle boxer; **Bryan Donkin** *(1768-1855)* – engineer and inventor.

Other names to look out for:
Sir Polydore de Keyser *(1832-97)* – first Catholic Lord Mayor of London since the Reformation, **Sir George Livesey** *(1834-1908)* – engineer and philanthropist; **Humphrey William Ravenscroft** *(1784-1851)* – wig-maker; **Thomas Tilling** *(1825-93)* – omnibus pioneer; **John Allen** *(1790-1865)* – ship-owner.

Plumstead Cemetery (1890)

Cemetery Road, off Wickham Lane, Abbey Wood SE2 0NS
Tel: 020 8856 0100
Transport: Welling Rail; Bus 96, 422, B11
Open: Daily 9am-7pm (Apr-Sept), 9am-4pm (Oct-Mar)

Plumstead Cemetery was originally laid out in 1890 on a prominent hillside that used to belong to Old Park Farm. The cemetery, which backs onto Bostall Wood, has a superb arched gateway and a driveway leading up the hill to the chapels at the top. As at Greenwich, there is a marvellous view across London to be enjoyed on a clear day.

The brightly coloured glass windows of the chapels are an unusual architectural feature, and give the buildings a somewhat Gallic feel. The angle of the ground around the chapels is quite disconcerting, and gives the impression that you're on a clifftop – again something not common in London.

The most interesting monuments relate to those killed while at work in Woolwich Arsenal, including a pink granite obelisk north of the chapels erected to the memory of those who died in two incidents in 1903, known as the Guncotton and Lyddite explosions, when a total of 11 men died in horrific accidents.

Also buried here are **Albert Gorman** and **Sir Edwin Hughes**, both former Mayors of Woolwich, Gorman having served 1940-41 and Hughes 1900-01. There is also a war hero – the Victoria Cross medal was awarded to **Alfred Smith** for saving Lieutenant D J Guthrie when the Camel Corps was on its way to relieve General Gordon, under siege at Khartoum.

Royal Hospital Cemetery, Greenwich (East Greenwich Pleasaunce) (1857)

Chevening Road, SE10 0LB
www.fegp.org
Transport: Westcombe Park Rail; Bus 108, 177, 180, 286
Open: Daily 7.30am-9pm (Apr-Aug), 7.30am-5pm (Sep-May)

The Royal Hospital for Seamen was founded in 1694. At that time seamen were buried in one of two burial grounds – one near the Dreadnought Seamen's Hospital, the other on Maze Hill which was used from 1707 to 1749, but remained in use for officers and children from the Hospital school until 1821.

The modern-day cemetery in East Greenwich is a formal, tree-lined garden which was opened in 1857. It was named 'Pleasaunce', after the royal palace known as the Palace of Pleasaunce, where King Henry VIII was born in 1491.

The Hospital became the Royal Naval College in 1873, and two years later the remains of some 3000 pensioners were moved from the old naval burial grounds to make way for the railway. Their memorial tablet reads: 'They served their country in the wars that established the naval supremacy of England and died the honoured recipients of her gratitude'.

The cemetery was sold to Greenwich Borough Council in 1926, and continued to be used for naval burials until the 1960s. One interesting remnant of the past is that men are buried in separate areas according to rank – officers in the east plot, Joe Sailor in the west.

The cemetery now serves more as a public park than a cemetery, complete with pleasant café and kid's play area, although the grave stones are still a visible testament to the park's naval history.

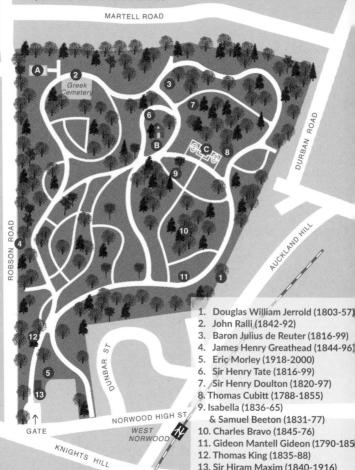

A) Old Garden of Remembrance
B) Chapel, Crematorium & Columbarium
C) New Garden of Remembrance

MARTELL ROAD

Greek Cemetery

ROBSON ROAD

DURBAN ROAD

AUCKLAND HILL

DUNBAR ST

GATE

NORWOOD HIGH ST

WEST NORWOOD

KNIGHTS HILL

1. Douglas William Jerrold (1803-57)
2. John Ralli (1842-92)
3. Baron Julius de Reuter (1816-99)
4. James Henry Greathead (1844-96)
5. Eric Morley (1918-2000)
6. Sir Henry Tate (1816-99)
7. Sir Henry Doulton (1820-97)
8. Thomas Cubitt (1788-1855)
9. Isabella (1836-65)
   & Samuel Beeton (1831-77)
10. Charles Bravo (1845-76)
11. Gideon Mantell Gideon (1790-185...
12. Thomas King (1835-88)
13. Sir Hiram Maxim (1840-1916)

West Norwood Cemetery (1837)

Norwood Road, SE27 9JU
Tel: 020 7926 7999
www.fownc.org
Transport: West Norwood Rail; Bus 2, 68, 196, 315, 322, 468
Open: Daily 8am-6pm (Apr-Oct), 8am-4pm (Nov-Mar),
 Sat & Sun from 10am
Guided tours (first Sunday of each month): 11am (Jan-Mar &
 Nov-Dec), 2.30pm (Apr-Oct)

West Norwood has survived bad maintenance, unplanned demolition and wartime bombing to become one of the most cherished cemeteries in London. Like its contemporaries north of the river at Kensal Green and Highgate, it was one of the 'Magnificent Seven' cemeteries, established in response to overcrowding in the city's churchyards. In keeping with contemporary aspirations, its Victorian financiers selected an elevated site with suitable topography to provide the public with somewhere they could be proud of spending eternity. December 12th 1837 saw the first burial at what was then known as the South Metropolitan Cemetery.

By the 1960s the cemetery was largely full and it was bought by Lambeth Council under a compulsory purchase order. Their 'lawn clearance' programme resulted in the removal of over 10,000 memorials. The destruction was stopped in the early 1990s when a Southwark church court judged it illegal, in part because West Norwood had originally been a private rather than a municipal cemetery. Further attempts to sell off the cemetery were thwarted in the late 1990s. The Friends of Norwood Cemetery's excellent newsletter tells how in September 2004 the family vault of noted writer and raconteur **Douglas William Jerrold** *(1803-1857)* was beautifully restored. Look out for that one.

Spring and summer bring a huge variety of flora and fauna to the landscape at West Norwood, and you can't really beat it as a venue for seeing foxes, owls, hawks and squirrels roaming wild so close to central London.

The cemetery certainly has no shortage of interest for the casual visitor, with 69 Grade II listed structures including several with fascinating historical associations.

Norwood has long had ties with London's Greek population, though the spread of the community northwards has meant that more recent graves are often found in the large Hellenic Enclosure at Hendon Cemetery. Nonetheless, the area of West Norwood reserved for Hellenes is nothing short of spectacular, with some of the cemetery's finest neo-classical monuments in a secluded north-eastern part that dates from 1842. The Ralli family of merchants built a Greek revival style chapel in 1872, and created a deceptively large mausoleum in honour of **John Ralli** *(1842-92)* and a Renaissance-style mausoleum for Eustratio Ralli around the same time.

Another nation with a large presence here is Germany, mainly due to the German church that once stood in nearby Forest Hill and the large German community at Denmark Hill. Journalists and reporters owe a great deal to **Baron Julius de Reuter** *(1816-99)*, founder of the Reuters news agency, commemorated here with a pink granite obelisk. Born Israel Beer Josaphat in Germany, he came to London aged 29 and progressed from using carrier pigeons to developing the first telegraph system in the 1860s.

A flat slab covered by an equally flat cross marks the tomb of **James Henry Greathead** *(1844-96)*, the engineer who designed the machine that bored the tunnels of the London Underground. His tunnelling shield was first used in 1869 and soon replaced the old 'cut and cover' system used in the earliest line (Paddington to Farringdon). His monument can be found outside Bank station, which was constructed using his machine. You can also find **Eric Morley** *(1918-2000)*, who became known as 'Mr World' due to his part in starting and popularising the world's leading beauty pageant, Miss World. From its humble origins as seaside beauty contests in Morley's Mecca dance halls, he developed a multi-million dollar (and opinion-dividing) enterprise, not forgetting his catchphrase 'And here are the winners, in reverse order.'

Some of Norwood's residents' influence endures for posterity in Londoners' daily life. An ornate terracotta mausoleum houses **Sir Henry Tate** *(1816-99)*, the Lancastrian sugar merchant who in 1897 established the gallery on the site of the old Millbank prison that we now know and love as Tate Britain. His legacy lives on in everyday life not only in the nationwide chain of Tate galleries, but also in Tate and Lyle sugar. **Sir Henry Doulton** *(1820-97)* himself is another resident with a well-preserved, decorative terracotta mausoleum. In succession to his father **John Doulton** *(1793-1873)* – also buried at Norwood – he pioneered and developed the Doultonware pottery that keeps dinner parties alive from Hampstead to Blackheath and beyond. Behind the New Garden of Remembrance is the family vault containing the remains of builder and entrepreneur, **Thomas Cubitt** *(1788-1855)*. Cubitt was responsible for many of the grand Georgian squares of Pimlico and Belgravia and in so doing acquired a great fortune. He remains the only builder to have a London monument in his honour.

The inscription on **James Busby**'s headstone tells his story succinctly. As British resident in New Zealand, 'He drafted the treaty of Waitangi'. He was also among the first to introduce the grapevine to the continent. A fading, plain tombstone marks the patron saint of celebrity cooks, **Isabella Beeton** *(1836-65)*, universally known as Mrs Beeton, without whose book *Household Management* the likes of Delia and Nigella would have no livelihood. She died of puerperal fever at just 29, surprisingly young for someone associated with such a 'matronly' subject. She only really became well-known after her bereaved husband **Samuel Beeton** *(1831-77)*, buried alongside her here, published her writings in book form.

The tale of **Charles Bravo** *(1845-76)*, who can be found in square 87, is one of the more mysterious stories surrounding the residents of West Norwood. He was a barrister whose agonizing death from poisoning at his house in Balham became the subject of the 'Balham Mystery' in William Roughead's book, *Classic Crime*. Either way, the case remains unsolved and the subject of enduring speculation.

Close by is the substantial railed sarcophagus marking the resting place of renowned paleontologist **Gideon Mantell** *(1790-1852)* who identified numerous dinosaurs and acquired a vast fossil collection. Mantell was a brilliant scientist, but suffered from financial problems forcing him to sell his collection to the British Museum in 1838. His wife left him the following year and in 1852 he suffered a terrible spinal injuring following a carriage accident. These misfortunes did not impede his studies, but his use of opium to control the pain of his injuries eventually resulted in an overdose in 1852. He left behind a vast body of work and a collection that can still be seen today.

Docker-cum-boxer **Thomas King** *(1835-88)* was born in Stepney, and while at work his quickfire destruction of a renowned dockyard bully called 'Brighton Bill' brought him to the attention of boxing promoters and led to his nickname 'The Young Sailor'. His best remembered fight was when he won a 25-round tussle against a far weightier opponent, the American John Camel Heenan in 1863.

Finally, a must-see here is a man indirectly responsible for helping to fill cemeteries worldwide – **Sir Hiram Maxim** *(1840-1916)*, the man the world can thank for the invention of the portable, fully automatic machine gun in 1884. Much less remembered is that he also experimented with powered flight without any success, though his Captive Flying Machine brought the crowds flocking to the Crystal Palace and elsewhere.

Notable Residents:

Douglas William Jerrold *(1803-57)* – author; **John Ralli** *(1842-92)* – merchant; **Baron Julius de Reuter** *(1816-99)* – news agency founder; **James Henry Greathead** *(1844-96)* – pioneering railway engineer; **Eric Morley** *(1918-2000)* – founder of Miss World; **Sir Henry Tate** *(1816-99)* – sugar magnate; **Sir Henry Doulton** *(1820-97)* – pottery manufacturer; **Thomas Cubitt** *(1788-1855)* – builder; **Isabella** *(1836-65)* and **Samuel Beeton** *(1831-77)* – author and publisher respectively; **Charles Bravo** *(1845-76)* – barrister and murder victim; **Gideon Mantell** *(1790-1852)* – paleontologist; **Thomas King** *(1835-88)* – boxer; **Sir Hiram Maxim** *(1840-1916)* – gun-making pioneer.

IN
LOVING MEMORY
OF
THOMAS KING
OF CLARENCE HOUSE
CLAPHAM PARK
DIED 4TH OCTOBER 1888
AGED 52 YEARS

Woolwich Cemetery (1856)

Kings Highway, Plumstead, SE18 2DS
Tel: 020 8856 0100
Transport: Welling Rail; Bus 51, 96, 422
Open: Daily 9am-7pm (Apr-Sept), 9am-4pm (Oct-Mar)

Woolwich Cemetery is in two parts, west and east, situated on either side of Rockcliffe Gardens. It was founded in 1856 on a 12 acre site which was formerly part of Plumstead Common. The west site has been adapted into a park like cemetery. Its hillside position offers cross-city views on sunny days, and it boasts an abundance of mature trees and a fine brick Anglican chapel on the brow of the hill.

Moving through the west cemetery, the most striking monument is a white marble Celtic cross commemorating 120 of those buried here who died in the *Princess Alice* disaster on the Thames on 3 September 1878. It remains the worst peacetime disaster to strike London's river, when the collier steamer *Bywell Castle* collided and cut the pleasure steamer *Princess Alice* in two. Of the 700 people on board only 69 survived – those who died were actually poisoned rather than drowned, due to the polluted state of the Thames. The inscription on the plinth tells the story in strangely quaint, formal language: 'it was computed that 700 men, women and children were on board.' The disaster caused a national outcry and almost certainly hastened the establishment of sewage treatment plants for the Thames. The cross was subsequently erected by a National Sixpenny Subscription to which over 23,000 people contributed.

The west site also features a memorial cross to **Temple Leighton Phipson-Wybrants**, who died in command of an expedition exploring the Sabi River in East Africa in 1880. His body was brought back at his mother's instigation and buried here in October 1881.

There is less to see in the newer eastern cemetery, but it's worth seeking out the odd but compelling sculpture of **Sister Gladys Richards-Lockwood** (d.1955) shown with spectacles and wearing her nurse's uniform.

SISTER GLADYS M.
RICHARDS-LOCKWO
S.R.N.   Q.A.I.M.N.S
30·8·1955·

OF ALFRED JAMES GILL

& CAPT. J. WARNE.

Such is Life!

East

Jewish Cemeteries in the East End

Chingford Mount Cemetery (1884)

Mount Cemetery, 121 Old Church Road, E4 6ST
Tel: 020 8524 5030
Transport: Chingford Rail; Bus W16, 158, 97
Open: Mon-Sat 7.30am-4pm, Sun 10am-4pm (Oct-Mar); Mon-Sat
   7.30am-7.30pm, Sun 10am-6pm (Apr-Sept)

Chingford Mount Cemetery was opened in May 1884, by the same company that set up Abney Park cemetery in Stoke Newington, after the latter became too congested. After many years of neglect by various private owners, it was taken over by the London Borough of Waltham Forest in 1977 shortly after it narrowly survived a proposal to replace it with new housing.

Much of the cemetery is laid out with traditional type full-size memorials and public graves. The granite beehives of the Norwood family tombs are one of the highlights here, but look somewhat out of place among the ubiquitous low-level white marble around them.

Many people go to Chingford for one family in particular, East End gangland legends the **Krays**. The cult of personality that built up around the twins Reggie *(1933-2000)* and Ronnie *(1933-95)* – sentenced to life imprisonment in 1969 – started with David Bailey's iconic 60s photographs, continued through the 1990 biopic starring Spandau Ballet's Kemp brothers and shows no sign of abating. The flowers and cards still arriving at Chingford Cemetery years after Reggie's death, bear witness to the enduring fascination with the Kray clan. In fact, all three brothers lie here, the twins and **Charlie** *(1927-2000)* as well as their beloved mother **Violet** *(1910-82)*, father Charles and Reggie's wife Frances.

Despite their sometimes being portrayed as lovable rogues, it's hard to pretend that the twins were gentle giants when faced with the hard, cold facts – George Cornell shot at point-blank range in the Blind Beggar pub (see Camberwell New Cemetery on page 158 for Cornell's grave), Jack 'the Hat' McVitie stabbed and impaled on floorboards, as well as a catalogue of intimidation in the East End. Still, 'they only killed their own' is the oft-repeated mantra, and brother Charlie's version of events could almost serve as a useful epitaph to his brothers: 'Sure the twins killed people. But they was in the twins' orbit. What I'm saying is, it wasn't normal people the twins done.'

Reggie was the last to go, in October 2000, released just weeks before his death from cancer. He had served over 30 years despite all his accomplices having long been set free. His hearse bore the message 'Free at last.' Ronnie and Reggie's grave is marked by a black marble headstone that says simply 'Legend', in gold leaf.

RAF pilot **Ernest Dobbs** *(1901-27)* lies nearby, killed at just 26 while balloon jumping in 1927. His stone reads ruefully: 'In science, he leaped to fame and, in the cause, he met his death'.

Looking at the cemetery as a whole, as elsewhere, the Victorian grandeur has long been superseded by utilitarianism and all memorials since 1981 are pretty standard. The newer areas are laid out in lawn type cemetery style, and lack real character.

Nonetheless, the wildlife is superb here. The main drive is lined with mature London plane trees, and the abundance of trees all around makes the cemetery attractive to the local squirrel community in particular.

Notable Residents:
Charlie Kray *(1927-2000)*, **Ronnie Kray** *(1933-95)*, **Reggie Kray** *(1933-2000)*, **Violet Kray** *(1910-82)* – members of Kray family; **Ernest Dobbs** *(1901-27)* –parachuting pioneer.

City of London Cemetery (1856)

Aldersbrook Road, E12 5DQ
Tel: 020 8530 2151
www.cityoflondon.gov.uk/things-to-do
Transport: East Ham LU, Wanstead LU; Bus 25, 86, 101, W19
Open: Mon-Fri 9am-7pm, Sat-Sun 9am-5pm (summer);
    daily 9am-5pm (winter)

City of London Cemetery really is a marvellous example of how a Victorian cemetery has managed to survive true to its original plan, combining tree-lined avenues with grand monuments amid the wonderful sweep of urban parkland. The paradox is that among such beauty and tranquillity, so many of its memorials are testament to the rough, tough and frequently grisly history of this part of London.

The cemetery probably benefited from having been established a few years after the establishment of the Magnificent Seven in the 1830s and 40s, enabling the planners to pick out the most successful features of the likes of Kensal Green and Abney Park. Its mastermind was William Haywood, at that time Surveyor and Engineer to the City of London Commissioners of Sewers.

Haywood noted in an 1849 report to his bosses that conditions in the City were pretty squalid, not least because there were 88 churchyards within the square mile alone, most of them in a dilapidated, overcrowded and gruesome state. Some were forced to close, and as a result Haywood began to look for a site for a new cemetery. In 1854 Aldersbrook Farm in Ilford was purchased from Lord Wellesley, a cousin of the Duke of Wellington, and Haywood was commissioned to design the new cemetery.

It opened in 1856, and remains a rare example of a cemetery that has been landscaped sensitively, with equal consideration given to practicality, aesthetics and posterity. Haywood laid out long, resplendent Parisian avenues with an air of the Champs Elysées about them, lining them with chestnut, lime and cedar trees.

There are eight Grade II listed buildings, and the entire cemetery itself is a Grade II registered Park and Garden of Special Historic Interest. Haywood's design included an extensive network of curving paths and avenues as well as two Gothic chapels and a valley of mysterious catacombs built into the banks of a former lake.

The opulent entrance still has its original ornamental iron gates, flanked by the porter's lodge. **William Haywood** *(1821-1894)* himself was buried in the cemetery when he died in 1894, and his gated, arched mausoleum can be found close to the main entrance.

The terrain is so vast and overwhelming that it is not surprising that the most striking sights are spread far and wide. Some monuments do stand out, such as a Gothic memorial to children from the local Royal Orphanage. The memorial to musician **Gladys Spencer** *(1897-1931)* is impressive – her grave features a female figure draped dramatically over a carved grand piano (see opposite).

Several areas were set aside to contain the reburied remains from many of the City churchyards closed and cleared when the City was rebuilt in the late 19th century. There are also reburials from churches destroyed as a result of bombing in the Second World War.

Equally fascinating for anyone with an interest in the darker side of London's history are the re-interred remains from Newgate prison burial ground after that was demolished in 1900, and the communal graves for 17th-century plague victims. Elsewhere, there's also a black marble stone for poor **Mary Ann Nichols** *(1845-88)*, who became one of Jack The Ripper's victims on 31 August 1888. Seek out the twin roundels marked 'Heritage Trail' for both Nichols and **Catherine Eddowes** *(1842-88)*, whose horizontal slab starkly and unambiguously states 'Here Lie Her Remains – Victim Of Jack The Ripper'.

On a less macabre note, another floor-mounted Heritage Trail roundel commemorates Victoria Cross recipient **John Joseph Sims** *(1835-81)*, a Crimean War hero who in 1855 rescued a group of wounded soldiers under heavy fire. Another notable tomb belongs to **George Micklewright** (1817–76), a

Grave of Gladys Spencer

conservationist considered to be the man responsible for saving Epping Forest in the late 19th century.

A crematorium was established here in 1903, a year after Golders Green had become the first in England. A Gothic framework hides its 80-foot chimney. In 1973 a second crematorium, with two chapels and six cremators able to deal with 40 funerals a day, was opened by the Lord Mayor. Here you can find a memorial to England's only World Cup-winning captain **Bobby Moore** *(1941-93)*, who died in 1993 from cancer and whose ashes were spread in the Gardens of Remembrance.

Sir Elwyn Jones *(1909-89)* deserves a special mention as not only an important local figure – he was MP for West Ham South from 1945-74 – but an instrumental prosecutor at the infamous Nuremberg trials in 1946. He was later made Lord Chancellor, a post which he held until 1979.

City of London Cemetery remains a potent symbol of the East End and differs from some of the earlier, Magnificent Seven cemeteries in its social diversity. While the original Victorian cemeteries were partly aimed at enabling the great and the good to be remembered for posterity, this cemetery has always catered for all spectrums of society. This is one of the reasons it is a place much beloved by locals.

With wide avenues lit by traditional street lights in the winter, grand Victorian memorials and a rolling landscape of lush greenery, the City of London Cemetery is a wonderful place to take an afternoon stroll. It also has a friendly little café next to the main entrance, which is a great place to relax after your exertions.

Notable Residents:

William Haywood *(1821-94)* – surveyor; **Gladys Spencer** *(1897-1931)* – musician; **Mary Ann Nichols** *(1845-88)* and **Catherine Eddowes** *(1842-88)* – victims of Jack the Ripper; **John Joseph Sims** *(1835-81)* – soldier; **George Micklewright** *(1817-76)* – conservationist; **Bobby Moore** *(1941-93)* – England football captain; **Elwyn Jones** *(1909-89)* – MP and Nuremberg prosecutor.

East London Cemetery (1872)

230a Grange Road, E13 0HB
Tel: 020 7476 5109
Transport: West Ham LU/Rail; Bus 69, 276
Open: Mon-Fri 9am-5pm, Sat-Sun 10am-4pm

Following the success of garden cemeteries in other parts of London, including nearby Tower Hamlets, East London Cemetery opened in 1872 with the aim of providing a burial ground for the local population of East London.

The original main entrance consists of stone piers and elaborate cast iron double gates, with pedestrian entrance gates on either side. Both Gothic chapels can be found in the centre of the cemetery, with one used by the crematorium, which was added in 1954, together with an ornamental rose garden. Paths are laid out symmetrically making the cemetery easy to navigate.

One of the bizarre features of East London is the amount of memorials to industrial catastrophes. One plinth commemorates the worst civilian disaster in British history, when over 600 perished after the paddleboat *Princess Alice* sank in 1878 in the Thames near Beckton. Many of the victims were killed not by drowning, but from the river's sewage pollution which at that time was discharged untreated from the Northern Outfall Sewage works nearby.

Directly facing the entrance, it's hard to miss the ship's anchor which commemorates those who were killed during the launching of *HMS Albion* in 1898, when the staging collapsed.

The Silvertown Explosion is commemorated in the grave of Andrea Angel, chemist at the Brunner Mond chemical works which exploded in 1917, killing 73 people and seriously injuring over 450, as well as causing the then gigantic sum of £2.5 million worth of damage. The cemetery also has a memorial erected in 1927 to all the Chinese who had died in England, and features a higher than average number of Oriental graves for a London cemetery.

There are also many actors buried at East London cemetery – few household names, but several that were familiar faces from 1960s and 1970s television. Character actor **Michael Barrington** (1924-88) was best known as the governor in classic BBC comedy *Porridge*, while **Christopher Blake** *(1949-2004)* was one of the stars of the successful 1977 adaptation of H E Bates' *Love for Lydia* and later the less successful but well intentioned sitcom *Mixed Blessings*, about a mixed race couple. Blake later become a scriptwriter until his death at just 54 from cancer. Look out too for TV favourites **Beryl Cooke** *(1906-2001)*, **Tony Steedman** *(1927-2001)* and **Arthur Howard** *(1910-1995)*, all of whom were regulars on TV in the three-channel era.

Most famous of all though was **Jack Warner** *(1895-1981)*, a man who made the expression *'Evenin' All'* synonymous with the London bobby in his definitive role as TV policeman *Dixon of Dock Green*. Warner's fame as Dixon eclipsed any of his previous work, which included a roles in the classic *The Ladykillers*. He continued as Dixon until his mid-70s, despite by then being quite an elderly man and not really a plausible bobby. The final series in 1976 saw him in a desk role, essentially narrating the story.

Notable Residents:

Michael Barrington *(1924-88)* – actor; **Christopher Blake** *(1949-2004)* – actor; **Beryl Cooke** *(1906-2001)* – actor; **Tony Steedman** *(1927-2001)* – actor; **Arthur Howard** *(1910-95)* – actor; **Jack Warner** *(1895-1981)* – 'Dixon of Dock Green' actor.

Manor Park Cemetery (1874)

Sebert Road, Forest Gate, E7 0NP
Tel: 020 8534 1486
www.mpark.co.uk
Transport: Manor Park Rail; Bus 101, 104, 308, 330, W19
Open: Mon-Fri 9am-7pm, Sat-Sun 10am-6pm (Apr-Sept), Mon-Fri
    9am-5pm, Sat-Sun 10am-4pm (Oct-Mar)

Manor Park Cemetery and Crematorium was opened in 1874 on
the eastern part of what had been Hamfrith Farm. The cemetery
today has two areas of woodland, the largest being in its north-
east corner where many woodland birds are to be found. The
original chapel, built in 1877, was largely destroyed by bombing
in 1944 apart from its spire which still remains, and was rebuilt
in brick with a crematorium added to its east end in 1955. The
cemetery also has a war memorial together with an extensive
Garden of Remembrance.

The very first incumbent at Manor Park, William Nesbitt, still
has pride of place on the right-hand side of Remembrance Road.
His grave bears the date 25 March 1875.

No less than two First World War holders of the Victoria Cross lie
here. **John Travers Cornwell** *(1900-16)* became the second youngest
holder of the medal at just 16, posthumously awarded for gallantry
at the Battle of Jutland in 1916, while **Sidney Godley** *(1889-1957)*
was one of the first soldiers to be awarded it after war broke out in
1914. Cornwell is buried in a family plot that features a tall cross
framed by a white anchor which is still well maintained. Also look
out for **Mary Orchard** *(1830-1906)*, whose monument was erected
'in grateful memory' by the four children of Queen Victoria's second
daughter Princess Alice. For forty years Mary looked after the
Princess's children, the youngest of whom, Alexandra (Alix), became
Empress of Russia on her marriage to Tsar Nicholas II.

Notable Residents:

John Cornwell *(1900-16)* – war hero; **Sidney Godley** *(1889-1957)* –
war hero; **Mary Orchard** *(1830-1906)* – royal nanny.

St Patrick's Catholic Cemetery (1868)

Langthorne Road, Leytonstone, E11 4HL
Tel: 020 8539 2451
Transport: Leyton LU; Bus W15, 58, 69, 97, 158, N26
Open: Mon-Fri 8am-4pm, Sun 9am-4pm (Winter); Mon-Fri 8am-
   5pm, Sun 9am-5pm (Summer)

The Central Line runs alongside St Patrick's Cemetery, providing commuters from east London a perhaps unwelcome reminder of their own mortality. The cemetery was founded in 1868 at a time when the 'Irish Question' was still a major issue in British politics, and was one of the few cemeteries in the country providing consecrated ground for Catholic burial. There have always been large Catholic communities in London and St Patrick's has proved a popular cemetery with over 170,000 souls now at rest within it's grounds.

In contrast to cemeteries such as Nunhead or Greenwich, there are hardly any trees to disrupt the open landscape of gravestones. In some parts of the cemetery soil has been placed upon older unmarked graves to create more space for the recently departed.

There is incredible diversity at St Patrick's with Catholics from across the world sharing this hallowed ground and expressing their faith in remarkably different ways. The figure of St Patrick holding a shamrock can be found here but so too can St Andrew, St Andrea, St Peter and Our Lady of Sorrows (Mary with seven daggers representing her suffering). Amid all the traditional Catholic statuary the Ferrari Mausoleum stands out as a concrete modernist structure. It was built in 1965 to house Lucia Ferrari, described as 'Mamma Adorabile'.

The Royal Marriages Act (1772) has long prevented Catholics from marrying into the royal family, but that has not stopped many of that faith giving their lives for 'King and Country', with numerous war graves and a dedicated area for Catholic soldiers killed in World War I.

St Patrick's may be a rather bare and exposed to the elements but it is still a cemetery with a unique character and with many tales to tell.

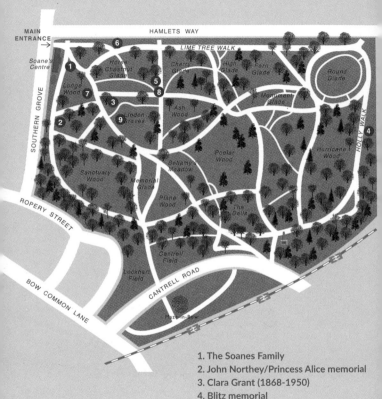

1. The Soanes Family
2. John Northey/Princess Alice memorial
3. Clara Grant (1868-1950)
4. Blitz memorial
5. Westwood monument
6. Walter Gray
7. John Willis (d.1921)
8. Joseph Westwood (1844-98)
9. Charlie Brown (1860-1932)

Tower Hamlets Cemetery Park (1841)

Southern Grove, E3 4PX
Tel: 020 8983 1277
www.fothcp.org
Transport: Mile End LU; Bus D6, D7, 25, 277, 339
Open: The park is open to the public 24/7

Tower Hamlets Cemetery Park's 31 acres of greenery makes it the largest woodland area in east London. It was set up by some of the wealthiest men of the Victorian age, yet it has the most urban and working-class history of all London's Magnificent Seven cemeteries. The parallels with today's Tower Hamlets – where the skyline of Canary Wharf sits uncomfortably alongside one of the poorest inner-city areas in the UK – are clear.

It ceased to be a working cemetery in 1966, and was thereafter transformed into a cemetery park, with ponds, meadows and woodand. Densely packed with graves and verdant with lush vegetation, the cemetery has acquired a reputation as a protector of the environment through its wildlife nature reserve, environmental education work and regular events programme.

Originally called The City of London and Tower Hamlets Cemetery, it was opened by a company made up of eleven directors whose occupations reflect the industries of the day: corn merchant, merchant ship broker and ship owner, timber merchant, and the Lord Mayor of London himself. It was originally divided into consecrated land for Anglican burials, and unconsecrated for other denominations. The first burial in 1841 was Walter Gray of Bow, who was interred in a private grave – unlike the vast majority of locals buried here too poor to afford a plot, funeral and memorial. Gray's plot is marked by a worn stone leaning against the railings on the right as you enter the main gates on Southern Grove.

By 1889, a quarter of a million burials had taken place here, but the nature of such public graves meant that few were tended regularly, many fell into neglect and the cemetery quickly became overcrowded. The cemetery was eventually closed for burials in 1963 and became a park three years later. Ownership was passed between councils until Tower Hamlets took over its running in 1986. Four years later, the Friends of Tower Hamlets Cemetery Park was set up and since then the group has helped transform the overgrown wilderness into something worth visiting.

In 2000, seven graves of outstanding design were given a Grade II English Heritage listing, and the following year the cemetery was declared a Local Nature Reserve. Many of the tombstones testify to the often precariously dangerous occupations of the local populace. Not surprisingly, sailors, mariners and dockyard workers are well-represented, such as Captain Lusby of Hull, who was accidentally shot while on duty and poor fourteen-year-old Peter Slader, who drowned after falling from a mast in West India Dock.

The combination of urban brutality and tranquil nature is one of Tower Hamlets' great pluses. The Cemetery Park is now a Site of Metropolitan Importance for Nature Conservation, while no less than seven memorials are listed, as are the towering brick walls that surround the cemetery. One of the best things about Tower Hamlets Cemetery Park is the way its nature reserve is used to benefit the borough. The Soanes Centre, just inside the main gate, was opened in November 1993 by David Bellamy, and not only provides education facilities for local schools but is a fascinating place in its own right. Its green roof is an unusual feature, and right beside the centre is a pretty pond and a wetland habitat.

The cemetery was bombed five times during the Second World War, which damaged both the Anglican and the Dissenters' chapels. You can still see shrapnel marks on some of the graves right by the Soanes Centre. Shortly after the Soanes Centre, you will find the Soanes family plot to the left of the War Memorial. A short walk to the right of the memorial takes you to where lies John Northey, who died in the wreck of the *Princess Alice* in 1878 (see pages 184 and 196).

Turn left and keep walking until you see the monument to the 'uncrowned King of Poplar', **Charlie Brown** *(1860-1932)*. He ran the Railway Tavern close to the West India Docks, but was better known for the incredible collection of antiques and oddities he

PEACE

IN MEMORY OF
A DEARLY LOVED HUSBAND
BENJAMIN WILLIAM
WHO PASSED AWAY 10TH
AGED 79 YEA
LIVE IN THE HEARTS OF

ALSO
BELOVED WIFE AN
ADA WHIT
PASSED

IN LOVING MEMORY OF
A BELOVED HUSBAND AND DAD
WILLIAM GEORGE RICHES
WHO FELL ASLEEP 19TH AUGUST 1959
AGED 66 YEARS
A light is from our household gone
A voice we loved is stilled
A place is vacal in our home
Which never can be filled

had acquired as payments for drink from sailors – stuffed animals, priceless vases and statues among the treasures. His funeral in 1932 was said to be the biggest the East End had ever seen.

Behind Brown and to the left you'll see a grave shaped in the form of an open book to mark **Clara Grant** *(1868-1950)*, the 'Bundle Woman of Bow'. Her pioneering efforts to alleviate the poverty of the East End did not go unnoticed and she eventually departed this world with an OBE and a well attended funeral.

Follow Holly Walk beyond the pond, until you come to the memorial to the Blitz. It's a charming garden of remembrance containing 190 graves, all residents of Poplar who were victims of the earliest Luftwaffe attacks. Moving northwards again, and then south to Memorial Glade, seek out the Westwood Monument, commemorating eminent ship and bridge builder **Joseph Westwood** *(1844-98)*. Next to him is a new memorial for three of Dr Barnardo's own children buried at that spot. It is also a memorial to honour over 500 impoverished children buried in unmarked public graves. The monument made of Portland stone was erected by the Barnardo's Charity in December 2016 the open hands represent Dr Barnardo's and the Cockney Sparrow represents the children he helped and released back to the world.

Turn right, following the path between Linden Graves and Horse Chestnut Glade to the end and on your left is a monument of red granite to **John Willis** *(d.1921)*, another prominent shipbuilder. Willis was the owner of the legendary *Cutty Sark*, that is now one of the key visitor attractions of Greenwich.

The Friends have produced a Heritage Trail for the Cemetery Park, marked by a series of purple and gold metal way finders. The trail can be viewed from their website or you can buy the trail leaflet for £1 from the Soanes Centre when you visit.

Notable Residents:

Charlie Brown *(1860-1932)* – publican; **Clara Grant** *(1868-1950)* – School mistress and philanthropist; **Joseph Westwood** *(1844-98)* – ship and bridge builder; **John Willis** *(d.1921)* – Ship owner.

Walthamstow Cemetery (1872)

Queens Road, E17 8QP
Tel: 020 8524 5030
Transport: Walthamstow Queens Road Rail; Bus 58, 230, W19
Open: Mon-Sat 7.30am-4pm, Sun 10am-4pm (Jan-Mar, Oct-
Dec); Mon-Sat 7.30am-7.30pm, Sun 10am-6pm (Apr & Sept)

Walthamstow Cemetery covers 11 acres and was opened in October 1872. The two Gothic chapels and belfry are joined at right angles, and were designed by R.C. Sutton. There is also a lodge, coroner's court and various buildings erected by the Burials Board back in the cemetery's heyday.

There is only one truly impressive mausoleum, that of **Jack Williams**, one of the great socialists in London's history. Williams was a vehement defender of the exiled German revolutionary Johann Most and openly sold his banned *Freiheit* on the steps of the Old Bailey in 1882 as Most's trial for incitement was in progress.

The cemetery became full a while ago, and as is often the case, the lack of new arrivals has led to a gradual neglect of many of the family graves. The pleasant drinking fountain in the centre of the cemetery alleviates some of the cemetery's overall dreariness but, apart from the odd winged angel, there's not too much to get excited about here.

Notable Residents:

Jack Williams *(c1850-1917)* – revolutionary Socialist.

West Ham Cemetery (1857)

Cemetery Road, Forest Gate, E7 9DO
Tel: 020 3373 1193
Transport: Forest Gate Rail; Bus 25, 69, 86, 308
Open: Mon-Fri 9am-5pm (Mar-Oct), 9am-4.30pm (Feb & Nov),
    9am-4pm (Dec-Jan), Weekends 10am-3pm

West Ham Cemetery is somewhat like its residents – no-nonsense and straightforward. It extends to approximately 22 acres with many hundreds of graves featuring elaborate Victorian headstones connected to stone kerbs.

In 1857 a newly-set up West Ham Burial Board, after noting the success of neighbouring Tower Hamlets, purchased 12 acres of land for a new cemetery from Samuel Gurney, a Quaker and a relation of the prison reformer Elizabeth Fry. The cemetery was subsequently extended to its current 22 acres in 1871.

Although the Nonconformist chapel has been demolished the original Anglican chapel survives to this day. It is Gothic in style, built of ragstone and was designed by T. E. Knightley, who was also responsible for several East End churches. A small mock-Tudor lodge building is situated just inside the entrance gates. The emphasis was on creating good drainage and keeping costs low, so the cemetery's layout is a simple grid plan with interlocking pathways.

There aren't really any prominent monuments in what is essentially a grassy sea of stones. Seek out **Frederick Sell** and **Henry Vickers**, two of the 69 firemen killed in 1917 when the TNT plant of the Brunner Mond chemical works in Silvertown exploded. Their funeral was a memorable event with a procession stretching over a quarter of a mile.

The brick wall which forms the boundary with the adjacent West Ham Jewish Cemetery (see page 223) is low enough to allow views between the two.

Woodgrange Park Cemetery (1890)

540 Romford Road, E7 8AF
Tel: 01375 891 440
www.fowpc.co.uk
Transport: East Ham LU, Manor Park & Woodgrange Park Rail;
 Great Eastern (Crossrail); Bus 25, 86, 101, 104, W19
Open: Daily 9am-7.30pm (May-Aug), 9am-7pm (Apr & Sept),
 9am-5.30pm (Mar & Oct), 9am-4.30pm (Nov-Feb)

Woodgrange Park Cemetery is one of the cemeteries in London that has undergone something of a transformation. The cemetery has for many year been owned by a private company, who wanted to develop parts of the site and faced local opposition. The company eventually applied to Parliament and in 1993 *The Woodgrange Park Cemetery Act* was passed, which allowed residents to be exhumed and reburied to make way for 120 two-bedroom flats.

In 2000, as work began, some headstones were taken away for use in the TV soap *Emmerdale*. It was claimed that the use of these stones was actually saving them from being broken up, but that didn't stop it from becoming a local cause célèbre. The dead appear to have had the last laugh, as tales of ghostly revenge on the new residents started to emerge.

What remains of the cemetery is shrouded by undergrowth, however the new section for the reinterments, known as the Memorial Gardens of Remembrance, is supported by the Friends of Woodgrange Park Cemetery and is furnished with bushes, benches and more.

There are no particularly interesting tombs other than a few polished granite examples that line the drive. The most fascinating thing to see at Woodgrange Park can be found within the Muslim area – the unmarked grave of five of the terrorists slain in the failed 1980 siege of the Iranian embassy in London.

New Sephardi, Mile End

Jewish Cemeteries in the East End

The history of Britain's Jewish community is intrinsically bound to that of the East End, and it is here, often within a few streets of each other, that the earliest Jewish cemeteries in London can be found.

After over a century of being tolerated for their value as merchants, Jews were banished from England in March 1290, after their impoverishment through continued over-taxation made them a liability for an impatient King Edward I.

They were not able to return until March 1656, when England was in its short-lived interregnum republican period. With Spain's expulsion of the Jews, Oliver Cromwell granted a petition allowing the Sephardic Marrano community their freedom to worship and with it the right to have their own burial ground.

A few months into 1657, what became known as the Velho (Old Sephardi) was opened in Mile End Road, and forty years later a cemetery was established at Alderney Road for those Ashkenazim of central and eastern European origins. These two cemeteries are beyond doubt the oldest surviving genuine cemeteries in London and deserve special attention for this reason.

The majority of Jewish cemeteries in the East End can be found in and around Mile End Road, though most of them no longer keep conventional opening hours. It is best to call the numbers given here and arrange a time for a visit, or alternatively peek at them from any number of overlooking vantage points.

Brady Street Cemetery (1761)

Brady Street, E1 5DJ
Tel: 020 8950 7767
Transport: Bethnal Green LU, Whitechapel LU;
  Bus 25, 106, 254, D3
Open: By appointment

Brady Street may have been closed to new burials since 1858 but it remains a big draw, though chances to visit it are scarce. The back-to-back tombstones on 'Strangers Ground' – so called because it was intended for those who belonged to no specific congregation – are unusual for London. They exist where the graves were repeatedly covered with four feet of new earth to make room for more graves on top, once the cemetery had become full in 1790. The eerie, medieval effect is much like the famous Jewish cemetery in Prague.

The raised central area of the cemetery is caused by this process of adding later layers to make room for new arrivals. Famous names buried here include **Solomon Hirschel**, Chief Rabbi between 1802 and 1842 and merchant banker **Nathan Meyer Rothschild** (1777-1836). Rothschild helped fund the British government during the Napoleonic wars – a useful and necessary way for these outsiders to keep in favour with the British establishment.

Many of the grave stones are entirely in Hebrew, some also have English script, but only one grave has an effigy. This unusual grave commemorates welfare worker **Miriam Levey** *(1801-56)* who opened London's first soup kitchen for the poor, around the corner in Whitechapel. She may not have been as rich as the Rothschilds, but the size and grandeur of her tomb shows the high regard in which she was held.

Brady Street Cemetery is a fascinating place to visit, though you will need to contact the United Synagogue Burial Society at the above number to arrange a visit.

Alderney Road Cemetery (1696)
Alderney Road, Stepney E1 4EG
Transport: Stepney Green LU, Mile End LU; Bus 25

New Sephardi, Mile End (1733)
329 Mile End Road, E1 4NS
Transport: Stepney Green LU, Mile End LU; Bus 25

Old Sephardi, Mile End (1657)
253 Mile End Road, E1 4NS
Transport: Stepney Green LU, Mile End LU; Bus 25

Alderney Road is among the oldest cemeteries in England, let alone London, and was the first to cater specifically for Ashkenazi, or eastern European, Jews. Opened in 1696, it was enlarged in 1733. There is a good variety of inscriptions, though most of the stones are now not surprisingly decayed.

The two Sephardi cemeteries best reflect what kind of Jewish community existed in London prior to the influx from eastern Europe at the end of the 19th century. Sephardis are essentially the Jews who fled from the Inquisition in Spain and Portugal in the 17th century, as oppose to the Ashkenazis of eastern Europe. More comprehensive information can be found at this marvellous website: *www.ferdinando.org.uk/sephardi.htm.*

The Old, or 'Velho', cemetery is the oldest Jewish cemetery in England, and was the first to be set up after the Sephardi community successfully petitioned Oliver Cromwell to allow their re-admission to England. Its design precedes that of the Victorian garden cemeteries by almost 200 years, and as such offers a rare chance to reflect on the toll 17th and 18th century events took on the poor masses of London. The Great Plague of 1665 was devastating and infant mortality was generally very high – look out for the numerous graves marked 'El Angelito' which translated means 'little angel'. Unfortunately most of the inscriptions have now faded.

The horizontal gravestones are a feature of the Spanish and Portuguese cemeteries, and symbolize that all are equal – rich and poor, upper and lower-class. And there are some very significant names indeed here.

The man generally considered to be the founder of London's Jewish community, **Antonio** (also known as Abraham) **Carvajal** (1590-1659), can be found here, as can physician to King John IV of Portugal **Dr Fernando Mendes** *(d.1724)* and scholar and rabbi **David Nieto** *(1654-1728)*. Carvajal was probably born in the Canary Islands, and passed through Rouen in France before settling in London in 1632. In 1657 it was he who took the initial lease on this cemetery.

About 200 yards to the east, the New, or 'Novo', cemetery is still extant despite receiving all manner of damage. The original wall, dating from 1733, still runs along Mile End Road. In 1940 many graves were destroyed by the Luftwaffe, an event commemorated by a monument. In 1974, the original plot was sold to Queen Mary College for redevelopment, leaving just an adjacent plot, bought in 1849, which remains to this day containing 2000 or so graves.

To see the New Sephardi Cemetery, walk down Westfield Way into the staff car park behind Queen Mary's Faculty of Arts building. Here you will find a raised platform allowing you views across this unique burial ground.

New Sephardi, Mile End

East Ham Cemetery (1919)

Marlow Road, E6 3QG
Tel: 020 8950 7767
Transport: East Ham LU; Bus 101, 104, 300
Open: Sun-Thurs 9am-4pm, Fri 9am-3pm

Plashet Park Cemetery (1896)

361 High Street North, Manor Park, E12 6PQ
Tel: 020 8950 7767
Transport: East Ham LU; Bus 101, 104, 300
Open: By appointment

East Ham is a typically small cemetery, and dating from 1919 coincides with the moment East End Jews started to move north-westwards. It contains tallish white marble headstones, and has a white-washed prayer hall.

Plashet Park is a small, rectangular cemetery with a spartan atmosphere that derives mainly from the densely-packed, flower-less nature of the place, again reminiscent of Prague's Jewish cemeteries. There isn't even a prayer hall, thanks to the efforts of the Luftwaffe, and the few visitors that pass through (I saw none) have the wind to contend with even on a sunny day. To be fair, several of the gated marble structures look rather stately.

One of the noticeable things at Plashet is that, as at many Jewish cemeteries, there are numerous examples of people who felt obliged to change their name in order to integrate. Hence, for example, one Henry Dawson (died 1929, aged 51) – he doesn't sound Jewish... until you see the inscription below 'formerly Gershon Freedman' and all becomes clear.

The abandoned ambience of the place was hardly helped by the desecration it received in May 2003 when around 386 gravestones were pushed over and vandalized, causing extensive damage which is still visible today.

Plashet Park Cemetery

Rothschild Mausoleum

West Ham Jewish Cemetery (1857)

Buckingham Road, E15 1SP
Tel: 020 8950 7767
Transport: Forest Gate Rail; Bus 58, 69, 308
Open: By appointment

West Ham's main cemetery (see page 209) is fairly well maintained, full of grass, trees and flowers but, just next door, over the brick boundary wall stands a bleak contrast. Burned grass, decaying monuments and an eerie atmosphere pervades West Ham's Jewish cemetery. Over a century of neglect has given this place a sense of history and makes it one of the most worthwhile of London's cemeteries to visit.

The five-acre plot on which this cemetery stands was bought from the same Quaker bankers who funded the main West Ham Cemetery, when nearby Brady Street become full to overflowing. Its layout bears the signs of necessity rather than ambition with simple gravel paths and little vegetation.

Without doubt, the most impressive sight at West Ham is the magnificent Renaissance-style circular mausoleum designed by Sir Matthew Digby Wyatt for the eminent Rothschild family. It was commissioned by **Ferdinand** for his wife **Evelina de Rothschild**, who died in childbirth in 1866 aged just 27. The initials E. R. are to be found everywhere. Ferdinand *(1839-98)* went on to become MP for Aylesbury, and was later buried here alongside her. Other names found here are former Lord Mayors of London **David Salomons** *(1797-1873)* and **Sir Benjamin Phillips** *(1810-1889)*.

At the north end of the cemetery, space was made in 1960 to re-inter remains from the old and now vanished Hoxton cemetery, used between 1707 and 1878 by the Hambro synagogue.

West Ham's Jewish cemetery can easily be glanced at, as it adjoins the main cemetery, but is not so easy to visit. Nonetheless, it can be done, by contacting the United Synagogue Burial Society (see number above), ideally giving a day or two's notice.

Outer London

Alperton Cemetery (1914)

Clifford Road, Alperton, Middlesex HA0 1AF
Tel: 020 8937 5733
Transport: Alperton LU; Bus 79, 83, 224, 245, 226, 297, 487
Open: Daily 9am-4pm (Jan-Feb & Nov-Dec), 9am-5pm (Oct),
    9am-6pm (Mar), 9am-7pm (Apr & Sept), 9am-8pm (May-Aug)

Opened as the First World War began, Alperton is a pretty but featureless cemetery. It has a simple redbrick chapel with a Welsh slate roof and beautiful stained glass windows, giving it the appearance of a small but prestigious private school.

Lying between the Grand Union Canal and the Bridgewater Road, the cemetery is home to a nature reserve full of urban foxes, frogs and wildfowl. Its wildlife area also contains peculiar little bird boxes. Alperton is certainly a well-maintained cemetery, and its flat-lawned short avenues give it a neat, tidy feel.

The monuments are by and large unspectacular, though one to look out for is a white structure with three angular, banked stones for the Skinner family. The other one you can't really miss is the unusual sculpture of a uniformed schoolboy.

Alperton Cemetery did manage to make the news in 1998 when the badly burned, unidentified body of a man was found beside a child's grave. A can of petrol and a lighter were found at the scene.

Beckenham Crematorium & Cemetery (1880)

Elmers End Road, Beckenham, Kent BR3 4TD
Tel: 020 8658 8775
Transport: Birkbeck Rail, Elmers End Rail; Bus 75, 147, 354, 356
Open: Daily 9am-4.30pm (Oct-Mar), 8am-6.45pm (Jun-Sept)

This cemetery has undergone considerable restoration work in recent years and contains many interesting memorials. It has a more rural feel than its address would suggest. An army of grey crosses in the undergrowth, resembling a wood in the middle of nowhere, is surrounded by trees disguising the fact that suburban south London lies a few metres on the other side.

The main chapel is a wonderful sight, with roses rambling over its roof and surrounded by all manner of overgrown forestry. A nearby stone commemorates 21 members of Beckenham's fire service, killed during one of London's heaviest air raids in April 1941. The crematorium features an ornamental waterfall In the midst of the series of plaques, and there are rose bushes in the Garden of Remembrance.

Once in the cemetery, sights are plentiful. The inscription 'Inventor and Sanitary Pioneer' tells visitors that they are now in the presence of **Thomas Crapper** *(1836-1910)*, the British innovator who brought flushing toilets to the Victorians. After years of neglect the monument on Crapper's grave was restored to its former glory in May 2002. Look for the Toblerone-shaped white marble tomb.

According to another tombstone, **William Walker** *(1899-1918)* is remembered for being 'The diver who saved Winchester Cathedral'. In 1905 several cracks appeared in the south and east sides of the cathedral and it was feared that the building might collapse. Due to waterlogging on the site, Walker was called upon to shore up the foundations of the crumbling edifice, diving up to six hours a day, often in darkness, for six years. From records kept at the time it is estimated that he used 114,900 concrete blocks

and 900,000 bricks. Once the job was done, Walker was awarded the MVO by King George V, who announced that he had 'saved the cathedral with his own two hands'. After surviving the ordeal Walker became a victim of the great flu epidemic of 1918. His renovated memorial is a modern black slab on an old grave and can easily be seen.

Frederick Wolseley *(1837-1899)* produced the first British motor-car and invented the sheep-shearing machine. Both feats are recorded on his black marble headstone, erected in 1988 by grateful sheep-shearing Antipodeans to celebrate Australia's bicentennial.

One of the medical profession's most colourful characters can also be found at Beckenham – none other than Dr William Gilbert Grace, better known as **W. G. Grace** *(1848-1915)*. Grace was probably the first superstar cricketer, though none would dispute that he is the most famous name from the game's pre-modern era. He scored a century in the first Test match ever played in England in 1880, and played international cricket until the age of 50 in a career that spanned 43 years. One famous apocryphal story tells how when Grace was unexpectedly bowled first ball, the umpire explained his decision not to give Grace out to the bowler with the words 'They have paid to see Dr Grace bat, not to see you bowl'.

Grace succumbed to a heart attack age 67 in 1915 while living just a few miles north at Mottingham. His grave lay neglected for much of the century until cricket writer David Frith led a successful campaign to have it restored and a new headstone erected. You can also visit a pub in nearby Anerley named in honour of the great man.

Notable Residents:
Thomas Crapper *(1836-1910)* – inventor of the modern lavatory; **William Walker** *(1899-1918)* – diver; **Frederick Wolseley** *(1837-1899)* – motoring pioneer; **W. G. Grace** *(1848-1915)* – cricketer.

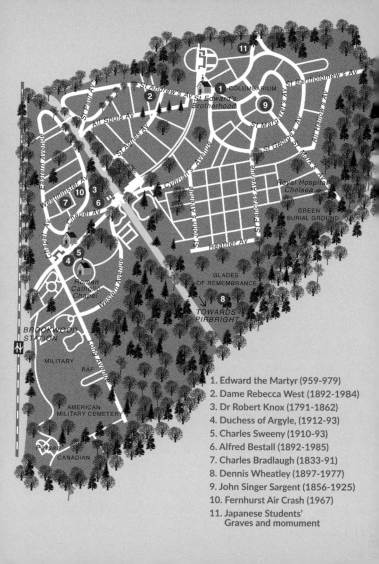

1. Edward the Martyr (959-979)
2. Dame Rebecca West (1892-1984)
3. Dr Robert Knox (1791-1862)
4. Duchess of Argyle, (1912-93)
5. Charles Sweeny (1910-93)
6. Alfred Bestall (1892-1985)
7. Charles Bradlaugh (1833-91)
8. Dennis Wheatley (1897-1977)
9. John Singer Sargent (1856-1925)
10. Fernhurst Air Crash (1967)
11. Japanese Students'
    Graves and momument

Brookwood Cemetery (1854)

Cemetery Pales, Brookwood, Woking, Surrey, GU24 0BL
Tel: 01483 472 222
www.brookwoodcemetery.com
Transport: Brookwood Rail (South West Trains from Waterloo)
Open: Daily 8am-5pm

Brookwood Cemetery is utterly unlike any other cemetery in this book. It isn't an oasis of tranquillity amid the noise of London – it's surrounded by a rural idyll already and lies some 30 miles outside Greater London. At the time of its consecration by the Bishop of Winchester in 1854, it was the largest cemetery in the world, and though it has since been overtaken, it remains the largest in the UK and is more than likely the biggest in Europe. Since 1854, over a quarter of a million people have been buried here, well in excess of any other cemetery in England.

Arguably, Brookwood is the cemetery that best sums up English society in its variety of creeds, cultures and classes and as such is of huge social and cultural importance and well worth a day out of town. A Home Office report in 2001 recommended that it be considered for a World Heritage Site status.

Despite the foundation of London's Magnificent Seven cemeteries, the sheer volume of London's dead proved to be an ongoing headache for the city's elders. An idea floated in 1850 suggested a great metropolitan cemetery located in the southern suburbs and large enough to contain an almost unlimited supply of London's dead. Almost immediately, the 'The London Necropolis & National Mausoleum Company' was born and was formally established by an Act of Parliament in June 1852. Bearing in mind that even the largest of London's cemeteries covers just 77 acres of land, the 500 acres that were set aside for the cemetery at Brookwood gives an idea of the scale of the enterprise.

One thing that arguably makes Brookwood such a fascinating place is not its famous residents (though there are some great names), nor its multiculturalism (though that is a superb feature), nor its wildlife and rural feel, nor even the sheer scale of the place.

No, the best feature of Brookwood Cemetery is that it had its own private railway, running into and out of the grounds, direct from London. The Necropolis Railway (see page 268) was the high-speed shuttle of its day, whisking Londoners to their tranquil final resting place.

The railway was no gimmick. With the cemetery over 25 miles from central London, the only viable way to transport coffins, mourners and officials from London was by train from Waterloo. At Brookwood there were two stations, North for the Nonconformists, South for the Anglicans. 1941 saw an end to the funeral trains from London due to extensive bomb damage to the terminus at Waterloo. The North station was demolished during the 1960s, but the South station survived as a refreshment facility for visitors until it was closed in 1967. The building was demolished a few years later but the platforms survive, although they are now no longer accessible to visitors.

Multiculturalism is a feature of Brookwood, with separate sections in the vast park for almost every conceivable group. It has the oldest Muslim cemetery in England, and a unique Zoroastrian burial ground. It also contains the largest military cemetery in the UK, with sections for Turkish, British, American, Canadian and Czechoslovakian war dead. The 'Glades of Remembrance', set up in 1950, is an area given over to those who have been cremated and wish to have their remains interred at Brookwood.

Brookwood may have lost its famous railway link to the capital, but it remains a fine example of a Victorian garden cemetery. The landscape is well cared for with avenues full of redwoods, pine trees, rhododendrons and wild flowers and enough notable residents to make it worth a day trip to explore.

Of the artists to be found at Brookwood, **John Singer Sargent** *(1856-1925)* is perhaps one of the most enduring names. A portrait painter at a time when Impressionism reigned supreme, it was only after his death that he became respected. Born in Florence, he worked mainly in Paris and London, where he created such works as *Portrait of Madame X*, in 1884. His grave can be seen in the area marked *The Ring*, in plot 35 near St Edward's Chapel, with the inscription, *Laborare est orare*.

One of the most fascinating and peaceful features of Brookwood is the small area in plot 39 commemorating four Japanese students who never actually met, but were all contemporaneous pioneers of Japan's post-feudal drive to explore the mysterious west, working 'for the modernization of Japan' as the inscription reads. The first to arrive, **Yamazaki Kosaburo**, died in London in March 1866 at just 22 after contracting tuberculosis. Three fellow Japanese students lie alongside Yamazaki, all of whom fell prey to illness and died young soon after reaching these shores. The tortuous journey to Europe, the alien environment and the incomprehensible diet could hardly have helped. The four men are linked by a monument put up in September 1977 by the Anglo-Japanese Friendship Association, 'in honor of their courage and their cause.'

Look carefully and you may find the small stone lying in solitude marked simply 'Anatomist' for medical pioneer and possible grave-robber's accomplice **Dr Robert Knox** *(1791-1862)*. In 1828 it emerged that Knox had been receiving corpses from Burke and Hare, who were at the time being prosecuted for murdering sixteen people to sell their bodies to medical researchers. Knox was eventually cleared of complicity, but his anatomy practice was never as big a draw again.

Close to Dr Knox can be found the Fernhurst Air Crash Memorial. It was on November 4th 1967 that an Iberia Airlines passenger jet destined for Heathrow crashed near the West Sussex village of Fernhurst, killing all 30 passengers and seven crew on board. Brookwood is not far from the crash site and it is here that 19 victims of the crash are buried around a pink granite obelisk commemorating the disaster. Each of the victims has a simple slate tablets bearing their name. The crash remains one of the worst in British aviation history.

Prolific writer **Dennis Wheatley** *(1897-1977)* can be found here too. Best known for his forays into the occult that made him one of the best-selling authors of the 1950s and 1960s, he also wrote books documenting real historical events and characters, such as the Russian Revolution and Charles II.

A bright, unusually tall headstone marks one of Brookwood's greatest love stories. **Margaret, Duchess of Argyll** *(1912-93)* and her first husband **Charles Sweeny** *(1910-93)* lie side by side, the society beauty and the once dashing American squadron leader and part-time golfer. Sweeny was a stockbroker who founded the American 'Eagle' squadrons that were based in England during the Second World War. One of the great society romances of pre-war England, he and Margaret divorced shortly after the war. Margaret then married the 11th Duke of Argyll before a scandalous divorce in 1963 – which involved photographic evidence of her infidelity being made public. Following the scandal, her wish to be buried at the Argyll family plot was refused, so she ended up being buried alongside Charles, her first love, who had died just weeks earlier.

The bones of a first-millennium English king, **Edward the Martyr** *(959-979)*, now lie at Brookwood. He met his end at the hands of his mother, Elfrida, who had preferred her younger son Ethelred ('the Unready') to be king. Legend has it that Edward's body was quickly hidden in a hut by Corfe Castle, Dorset before being discovered by a blind woman whose sight was apparently restored. Miracles were said to happen every time his body was moved thereafter, first to Wareham, then to Shaftesbury Abbey and Edward was canonised in 1008. An archaeological dig in 1931 confirmed the existence of the bones, in 1982 the Russian Orthodox Church became their custodians and they were duly enshrined in the Church of St Edward the Martyr in Brookwood Cemetery.

Children of all ages will want to see the circle-backed cross that marks the grave of **Alfred Bestall** *(1892-1985)*. He illustrated the *Rupert Bear* stories in the *Daily Express* from 1935 to 1965, writing over 270 Rupert adventures.

London's cemeteries contain a disturbing number of graves belonging to victims of the occasionally unjust British judicial system. **Edith Thompson** *(1893-1923)* is a case in point. In 1923

BURIAL GROUND

she was found guilty of her husband's murder – the only 'evidence' being love letters she'd written, wishing ill on her husband, that were most likely the fantasies of a bored housewife. Her memorial is a flat slab containing the names of a total of four women who were executed at Holloway prison. The stone remains, but in November 2018 her remains were removed and re-interred in the City of London Cemetery to lie with other members of her family.

The most recent notable arrival to Brookwood is the architect Zaha Hadid *(1950-2016)*. She was the first woman to receive the RIBA gold medal and went on to design buildings across the world from Baku to Berlin. Only a few examples of her work are to be found in her native London, the most famous being the Aquatic Centre for the 2012 Olympics. Hadid died suddenly from a heart attack in 2016 and is buried here alongside her father.

The Necropolis Company was dissolved in 1975, and despite various changes the cemetery remains in private hands. The Brookwood Cemetery Society has been doing a great job of promoting the interests of the cemetery since 1992, and keeps up a programme of ongoing maintenance, clearance and restoration work, as well as organizing guided tours, regular talks and the updating of its superb website – *www.tbcs.org.uk*.

Notable Residents:

John Singer Sargent *(1856-1925)* – artist; **Dr Robert Knox** *(1791-1862)* – medical pioneer; **Dennis Wheatley** *(1897-1977)* – novelist; **Margaret Campbell, Duchess of Argyll** *(1912-93)* – socialite and **Charles Sweeny** *(1910-93)* – American golfer; **Edward the Martyr** *(959-979)* – English king; **Alfred Bestall** *(1892-1985)* – illustrator of *Rupert the Bear*; **Edith Thompson** *(1893-1923)* – victim of miscarriage of justice; **Dame Rebecca West** *(1892-1984)* – writer and journalist; **Charles Bradlaugh** *(1833-91)* – Victorian social reformer; **Zaha Mohammad Hadid** *(1950-2016)* - architect.

Carpenders Park Lawn Cemetery (1954)

Oxhey Lane, Carpenders Park, Watford WD19 5RL
Tel: 020 8937 5733
Transport: Carpenders Park Rail (then 10-15 mins walk);
    Bus 8 (from Northwood/Watford), 350
Open: Daily 9am-8pm (May-Aug), 9am-4pm (Jan-Feb & Nov-Dec),
    9am-5pm (Oct), 9am-6pm (Mar), 9am-7pm (Apr & Sept)

Carpenders Park is a particularly eco-friendly cemetery, in a surprisingly rural area given its closeness to London. Grey squirrels and jays roam the lush woodland which is accompanied by a small lake housing ducks and kingfishers.

Only biodegradable coffins are allowed here in line with the cemetery's back-to-nature management of the woodland. Wooden coffins are allowed, but only if they come from managed forests. Since 1980 there has also been a Muslim burial area. One striking feature of the cemetery's lawn-type layout is that there are no upright memorials or headstones, just bronze plaques lying in the ground.

One plaque that is definitely worth looking for is that for **James Francis Hanratty** *(1936-62)*. Hanratty was a small-time crook found guilty of murdering civil servant Michael Gregsten, and raping and leaving for dead his lover Valerie Storie on the A6 near Bedford, in what became known as the 'A6 murder'. Hanratty denied the charge but in 1962 he became one of the last three men in Great Britain to be executed. Since his death his family have continued to campaign for his posthumous acquittal. He was first buried in 1966, but his body was briefly exhumed for DNA tests and reburied in March 2001. The DNA tests recently confirmed Hanratty's involvement in the crime. Hanratty lies alongside his aunt, Anne Cunningham (1895-1977), who campaigned tirelessly on his behalf.

Notable Residents:

James Hanratty *(1936-62)* – one of the last three men to be hanged in England.

Croydon Cemetery & Crematorium (1897)

Mitcham Road, Croydon, CR9 3AT
Tel: 020 8684 3877
Transport: East Croydon or West Croydon Rail;
    Bus 64, 109, 264, 289; Tramlink Therapia Lane stop
Open: Daily 9am-7pm (Apr-Sept), 9am-5pm (Oct-Mar)

Croydon Cemetery was enlarged in 1937 when the crematorium was built and in 1962 the understated east chapel was added. The memorial gardens are more attractive than most contemporary crematoria, being divided into well designed, split-level squares and are well-maintained, almost in the manner of a Japanese garden.

The main cemetery is by contrast a bland disappointment. One interesting memorial is a black granite cross set on a vast flower bed erected in 1962. It commemorates the thirty-four pupils and two masters from Lanfranc school who died in an air crash off the coast of Norway in August 1961.

Apart from an unusually high number of winged angels, a fading stone embedded with an anchor and the carving of a plane on the stone of Captain Leslie Thomas, there is not a great deal else until you spot the flowers surrounding the Bentley family plot. **Derek Bentley** *(1933-53)* lies here, the victim of possibly the worst, and best-known, miscarriage of British justice in modern times.

Bentley was an easily-led young man of limited intelligence. He was roped into a warehouse robbery by his 16-year-old friend Christopher Craig. Once cornered, Craig shot and killed one policeman, after Bentley had famously told him to 'Let him have it.' Craig got away with a jail sentence due to his age, while the older Bentley faced the gallows just weeks later.

Bentley's body was moved from the grounds of Wandsworth Prison in 1966, and reburied in Croydon Cemetery. Ironically, this was where the ashes of P.C. Miles, the murdered policeman, had been scattered.

Bentley's sister, Iris *(1931-97)*, fought for many years to clear his name but died a year before the Court of Appeal quashed his conviction. Her ashes were placed on his grave, in an urn, inscribed with the words 'The Truth Will Out' and later the words 'A victim of British justice' were added to Derek Bentley's tombstone.

Charles Cobb *(1878-1919)* was a victim of the First World War despite not actually going into battle. A conscientious objector, he was imprisoned five times between 1916 and 1919. Like many who made the same choice, he was subjected to harsh jail conditions which contributed to his death soon after his final discharge. His grave lay unmarked and neglected until 1988 when a marble headstone was erected by some of those sympathetic to his cause. The inscription on the stone 'I fear God, not man' is quoted from his first trial. In front of the new headstone are the graves of military dead, and not far away lies a memorial to the civilians of Croydon who were killed in the Second World War. A monumental broken cross marks the resting place of one of Britain's most promising composers, **William Yeates Hurlstone** *(1876-1906)*. He left a small body of quartets, sonatas and works for orchestra before his untimely death at the age of thirty from an asthma attack.

Burial space, as elsewhere, has been at a premium here for some time. Plans to build a high rise mausoleum in 2002 were scuppered due to objections to graves being moved. In April 2004, four hundred graves were reclaimed without serious objection because all the plots were over 75 years old. The reclaimed plots are now being used for new burials.

Notable Residents:

Derek Bentley *(1933-53)* – victim of British justice; **Iris Bentley** *(1931-97)* – his sister, and campaigner for his pardon; **William Yeates Hurlstone** *(1876-1906)* – musician and composer; **Charles Cobb** *(1878-1919)* – conscientious objector.

East Sheen Cemetery (1903)

Sheen Road, Richmond, TW10 5BJ
Tel: 020 8876 4511
Transport: Richmond LU/Rail, North Sheen Rail (South West
    Trains from Waterloo); Bus 33, 337, 493
Open: Daily 10am-6.30pm (Apr-Oct), 10am-4.30pm (Nov-Mar)

East Sheen and Richmond Cemeteries stand virtually side by side
and can easily be visited together. Although it is a relatively small
cemetery, East Sheen offers interesting sights and is one of the
best cemeteries for spotting members of the acting profession.

Just south of the chapel stands the cemeteries finest monument
– the hugely dramatic, bronze winged angel draped over the tomb
of **George William Lancaster.** It would be spectacular anywhere,
and looks as though it should be in a museum of art rather than
in a mere cemetery (see photograph on following page). The
Lancasters were a northern family who made their money in coal
mining and lived at Clare Lawn, the grandest of all the houses in
East Sheen. Their memorial was sculpted by Sydney March.

One other statue stands ruggedly out from the rest. Lording
it in a stone chair, the figure of **William Rennie-O'Mahony** sits
proudly, gun in hand, guarding his place of rest. He died from war
wounds in 1928.

In the centre of the cemetery you can find the Gothic-style
chapel designed by local architect Reginald Rowell, who is also
buried here. Just yards from the chapel, stand up straight and
look lively for **Fulton Mackay** *(1922-1987)*, the Scottish actor, best
known for his role as the prison officer in the sitcom *Porridge*. His
wife, actress Sheila Manahan, is buried beside him.

You will then notice a spectacular monument featuring a pair
of embracing dolphins. **Rosemary Gibb (Rosie)** was a children's
entertainer, and her spectacular memorial of a mother and child is
unusually made of wood and painted silver.

Another worthy name is **Edouard De Leon Espinosa** *(1871-1950)*
– the founder, with his wife **Louise** (d 1943), of the British Ballet
Organisation in 1930. Next up is a homely, gated tomb containing

East Sheen Cemetery

AND LOVING MEMORY OF

RGE WILLIAM

NCASTER

JANUARY 1920

GED 66 YEARS

E LIVES FOR EVER"

a severe-looking white cross for the Mawhinney family, inscribed 'in the garden of memory, we meet every day.'

A memorial to oddball music hall act **William Ellsworth Robinson** *(1861-1918)* stands in the southerly part of the cemetery. Robinson was a member of the Magic Circle, who renovated his monument in 1999. Known on stage as Chung Ling Soo, he became legendary for his act of catching bullets in his teeth. Not entirely surprisingly, he met his own end on the music hall stage, in apparently mysterious circumstances. Robinson was shot on stage performing the infamous 'bullet-catching trick', and died the following day. His death contributed to the compelling aura of superstition that has led numerous famed magicians to shy away from performing the trick. Even Houdini, who undertook seemingly death-defying defeats, listened to the counsel of Harry Kellar, and refrained from attempting the feat.

Just a few steps to the left lies a familiar name from the television age, much-loved comedian and actor **Roy Kinnear** *(1934-1988)*. Kinnear came to prominence as one of the original purveyors of television satire on the seminal 1960s show *That Was The Week That Was*. It was while filming Richard Lester's *The Return of the Three Musketeers* movie that Kinnear was thrown off his horse and developed complications after suffering a broken pelvis. His headstone is topped by a pair of actor's masks, and notes simply that he was 'tragically killed whilst filming in Spain'.

Notable Residents:

Fulton Mackay *(1922-1987)* – actor; **Edouard De Leon Espinosa** *(1871-1951)* – founder of the British Ballet Organisation; **William Ellsworth Robinson** *(1861-1918)* – magician; **Roy Kinnear** *(1934-1988)* – actor.

Forest Park Cemetery & Crematorium (2005)

Forest Road, Hainault, Essex IG6 3HP
Tel: 020 8501 2236
www.forestparkcrematorium.co.uk
Transport: Fairlop LU; Bus 150, 247, 362
Open: Mon-Sat 8am-8pm (Summer), 8am-5pm (Winter),
**   opens 10am Sundays**

This new addition to London's cemeteries opened on 1 February 2005, and has already become a symbol of the city's multi-faith, multi-cultural society at its best. It also represents London's perennial expansion outwards, and demonstrates the city's ability to cope with the relentless spread of its urban population.

A multi-faith service was held to mark the opening of the cemetery, which is located just opposite Hainault Country Park. More than a hundred people, representing several different faiths, attended the opening ceremony and dedication service in the well-designed chapel. The cemetery has separate burial areas for people of different faiths and includes Roman Catholic and Anglican sections, as well as offering Hindu and Sikh cremation services.

One reason why the new cemetery is of such interest is that it goes against the post-war decline in burials. The introduction to this book tells of how London is battling a severe lack of burial space, and some cemeteries have encountered difficulties when forced to reuse old burial space. Yet at Forest Park, the intention is clear – to provide the borough with enough burial space for at least the next 60 years.

Gardens of Peace
Muslim Cemetery (2002)

Elmbridge Road, Hainault, Ilford IG6 3SW
Tel: 020 8502 6000
www.gardens-of-peace.org.uk
Transport: Hainault LU, Ilford Rail; Bus 150 (from Ilford Rail)
Open: Daily 8am-7pm (Apr-Sept), 8am-5pm (Oct-Mar)

The largest Muslim cemetery in the UK was opened in Ilford in 2002, and since then has been nothing less than an overwhelming success story, and is well worth a visit whatever your faith. A registered charitable trust, the name 'Garden of Peace' is highly apt.

This cemetery is a fine example of what can be done if backing can be found for relieving the burden on burial space in the capital. It opened in time for Ramadan in 2002, and its 10,000 grave capacity makes it well-placed to meet the demands of east London's Muslim community for generations as yet unborn.

Islamic culture insists on burial rather than cremation, and graves should ideally be oriented towards Mecca. As a result, trees planted at the head of graves are designed to create a grid that faces the holy city. The majority of Muslim burials in the UK are in cemeteries run by local councils, and this can sometimes mean that Muslims are not always buried in accordance with Islamic law.

The Garden of Peace doesn't appear to feature any really overt Muslim imagery. It does however radiate a tranquil atmosphere, with its wide landscaped gardens, sizeable ponds, and a stream that runs through the centre. It has already won two international awards for its design and it will be intriguing to see how the landscape develops over the years.

On 15th July 2005 7,000 people attended the funeral of Shahara Islam, the first victim of the London bombings to be buried. She had been a passenger on the number 30 bus targeted by a suicide bomber on the morning of 7 July. As a Muslim herself, her killing was seen by many as a symbol of the futility of the bombers' efforts.

Greenford Park Cemetery (1901)

Windmill Lane, Greenford, UB6 9DR
Tel: 020 8825 6030
Transport: Greenford LU
Rail: North Greenford Rail (Thames Trains from Paddington);
    Bus 92, 282, E5
Open: Mon-Fri 8am-7.30pm (May-Aug), 8am-7pm (Apr & Sep),
    8am-5.30pm (Mar & Oct), 8am-4.30pm (Nov-Feb), open 9am
    weekends

Greenford is a busy, modern and colourful cemetery reflecting the multi-cultural nature of its local community. Its smart brick chapel looks like it has received a fresh coat of paint recently, and is obviously in good condition because it's being kept busy.

One particular monument worth going to see is that of a sportsman who died young – England cricketer **Wilf Slack** *(1953-89)*. Slack had been one of the most consistent batsman in England, and still had ambitions for a place on the England team when he suffered a fatal heart attack in early 1989. His black marble headstone features a wicket and the Middlesex county crest, and the message 'you bat on in our memories'.

One particularly charming tomb features a rather friendly-looking lion and the poignant message, 'Walk slowly Dad, I'll catch you up one day.'

In October 2003 the cemetery became the focus of national attention when it held the funeral of Heshu Yones, a young woman whose Kurdish Muslim father had murdered her in an 'honour killing'. He was said to have been angry about her burgeoning relationship with a Christian teacher. Mourners held a minute's silence at her grave, which was covered with candles and many bouquets of flowers.

Notable Residents:

Wilf Slack *(1953-89)* – England Test cricketer.

Isleworth Cemetery (1880)

Park Road, Isleworth, TW7 6AZ
Tel: 020 8583 6080
Transport: Syon Lane Rail (South-West Trains from Waterloo);
   Bus 117, 267, H28, R62
Open: Daily 24/7

Isleworth Cemetery, one of the smallest in and around London, opened in 1880 when the nearby riverside burial ground of All Saints became full. Its two large twin Gothic chapels are situated in a pretty setting of mature trees and shrubs but look like they have seen better days. Windows are boarded up, the brickwork could do with an overhaul and the withering octagonal spire is a sorry sight.

Right next door and overlooking the cemetery is West Middlesex Hospital, whose patients surely can't take much solace from the cemetery's proximity.

Notable amongst the memorials at Isleworth is the ornate polished granite structure in memory of the **Pears** soap dynasty, one of whom, Thomas, went down with the *Titanic* in April 1912. Pears soap factory was one of the area's major employers in the 19th century, and **Andrew Pears** *(1846-1909)* was a significant philanthropist of the time. The initials 'A. P.' can be seen on the lodge in the Grove. Andrew Pears's ashes were buried at Isleworth right by the family's memorial.

There is also a striking red granite obelisk to honour local girl Alice Ayres, who was killed saving three children from a fire in 1885. A plaque commemorating her courage can be found at Postman Park near St Paul's.

Notable Residents:

Andrew Pears *(1846-1909)* – soap magnate.

Morden Cemetery (Battersea New) (1891)

Lower Morden Lane, Morden, Surrey SM4 4NU
Tel: 020 8337 4835
Transport: Motspur Park Rail (South-West Trains from Waterloo);
   Bus 163, 293, 413, K5
Open: Daily 8am-4pm (Jan-Feb & Nov-Dec), 8am-5pm (Mar &
   Oct), 8am-6pm (Apr & Sept), 8am-7pm (May-Aug), Sun opens
   10am

Battersea New Cemetery, as it was originally known, opened
in 1891. Ecological concerns are pretty high here now, and
it has been declared a site of metropolitan importance for
nature conservation due to the variety of rare grasses and
wildflowers found here. It is also renowned for its profusion of
grasshoppers and crickets – in total, there are 110 species of
wildflowers and grasses and the site is also home to some 256
invertebrate species.

Noteworthy monuments are not plentiful, but there are one
or two. Irish-born Victoria Cross medal recipient **John Sinnott**
(1829-96) won his award at Lucknow in 1857 during the Indian
Mutiny, and is commemorated by a fading stone with carved
cups on either side.

Included within the cemetery's grounds is North East Surrey
Crematorium, established in 1958, which affords a very pleasant,
park-like stroll through lawns, rose gardens and rockeries. There
is a gorgeous colonnade in the remembrance gardens where it is
common to leave flowers.

There are worries about Morden's future because the
cemetery is on a flood plain and high rainfalls since 1999 have
caused some areas – in particular the Muslim burial area set up
in 1995 – to waterlog and deteriorate. As a consequence, the
local council has decided to build concrete burial chambers as
they fear that local Muslims will move their burials elsewhere if
flooding continues to damage their burial area.

Richmond Cemetery (1853)

Lower Grove Road, Richmond, TW10 5BJ

Tel: 020 8876 4511

Transport: Richmond LU/Rail), North Sheen Rail (South-West)
    Trains from Waterloo); Bus 33, 337, 493

Open: Daily 10am-6.30pm (Apr-Oct), 10am-4.30pm (Nov-Mar)

Richmond has been described as the Hampstead of the south. Both boroughs are remarkably green and pleasant places and both have fine cemeteries. In Richmond there are two cemeteries, with the smaller East Sheen (page 241) bordering the better known Richmond Cemetery. The latter has a decidedly rural feel, with plenty of flowers in bloom in the spring and summer and even some palm trees.

Richmond's origins lie in a section of land given by King George III to be set aside for burials, which eventually fell into municipal use once the Victorians were comfortable with the idea of garden cemeteries. One notable early step at Richmond was the rejection of divisions between consecrated ground (for 'believers') and unconsecrated ground (for 'Dissenters') – a wall erected to do just that in 1873 was soon torn down and not replaced.

The finest sight at Richmond is probably the white lion that guards the **Bromhead Memorial**, the monument to the Star and Garter Home for Disabled Sailors. Unveiled in 1957 by Field-Marshall Lord Alanbrooke, it commemorates those who died at the nearby home for ex-servicemen. A second monument was installed in 1994, a large elaborate cross in the middle of the cemetery.

Perhaps not surprisingly, given its extensive military heritage, Richmond is notable for the number of holders of the Victoria Cross buried here. Whatever your views of Britain's imperial past, the Victorian graves are well worth seeking out because they give an insight into that period of history when Britain was at its most powerful.

A carving of a cross lying on a pillow of stone marks the

memorial for **Sir Harry Prendergast** *(1834-1913)*, who served as a general in the Madras Engineers. His VC was awarded for his service during the Indian Mutiny in 1857. The same historical event garnered a medal for **Sir William Olipherts** *(1822-1902)*, a general in the Bengal Artillery at the Relief of Lucknow the same year. Look for the flat slab with a shield, a sword and at the head, a cannon motif similar to the old Arsenal FC badge. **Harry Hampton** *(1870-1922)* served as a colour-sergeant in the King's Liverpool Regiment. He was awarded his VC for service at Van Wyck's Vlei during the 2nd Boer War in August 1900.

It is also significant that the cemetery is a focal point for South Africans too. A section in the northern part of the cemetery was set aside in 1918 for a memorial designed by Sir Edwin Lutyens, whose glorious work can also be seen extensively at Golders Green Crematorium. The 15 feet high granite memorial was designed to bear a strong resemblance to the Cenotaph in Whitehall, another Lutyens creation.

On the memorial, you can see inscriptions in both English and Afrikaans which read 'Union is Strength' and 'To Our Glorious Dead'. It was unveiled by General Smuts in June 1921, but once the apartheid era really took hold, the South African government shunned the place and it was left to the Commonwealth War Graves Commission to maintain it.

It is not all military here though. There is also novelist **Mary Braddon** *(1835-1915)*, who translated Flaubert's *Madame Bovary* and whose novel *The Rose of Life* was based on the life of Oscar Wilde. She is often said to have been the founder of a new school of 'sensational' fiction, and her racy novel *Lady Audley's Secret* was dramatised by the BBC in 2000.

A poignant memorial alongside the main road commemorates two young sisters **Amy and Lily Hensen**, who died of Spanish flu in the 1918 epidemic. A white obelisk remembers radical political figure **George Julian Harney** *(1817-1897)*. Said to be the last of the Chartist leaders, Harney was fiercely active in radical politics, and frequently imprisoned.

He was a close friend of contemporary radicals Karl Marx and Friedrich Engels, and befriended Victor Hugo when both of them were forced into exile in Jersey.

No major cemetery is complete without a bizarre rock star casualty, and Richmond is no exception. **Keith Relf** *(1943-76)* came to prominence as the lead singer of sixties British blues-rock band *The Yardbirds*, best-known for hits such as *Heart Full of Soul* and *For Your Love* and for being home at one time or another to almost all the legendary British rock guitarists of the sixties. Relf died when he suffered a heart attack, reputedly caused by an electric shock from his home guitar amplifier – he was just 33. His grave can be found just east of the Star and Garter memorial.

Montague Summers *(1880-1948)* was an undeniably eccentric religious figure and author. He was a priest widely associated with witchcraft, who wrote extensively about demonology but spent much of his time denouncing it. His rectangular headstone reads 'Tell me strange things', which was apparently his usual opening gambit to strangers.

A path leads to the family cremation section, a colourful area in the south-east corner, while the well-tended Garden of Rest is just by the path that divides Richmond from East Sheen Cemetery.

Notable Residents:

Harry Prendergast *(1834-1913)* – soldier; **William Olipherts** *(1822-1902)* – soldier; **Harry Hampton** *(1870-1922)* – soldier; **Mary Braddon** *(1835-1915)* – novelist; **George Julian Harney** *(1817-1897)* – political radical; **Keith Relf** *(1943-76)* – *Yardbirds* vocalist; **Montague Summers** *(1880-1948)* – priest and author.

Sutton Cemetery (1889)

Alcorn Close, Oldfields Road, Sutton, Surrey, SM3 9PX
Tel: 020 8644 9437
Transport: Sutton Common Rail; Bus 80, 470, S3
Open: Mon-Fri 8am-8pm (May-Aug); 8am-7pm (Apr & Sep);
    8am-5pm (Feb-Mar & Oct); 8am-4pm (Nov-Jan),
    opens 9am weekends

Sutton Cemetery was established in 1889, and is owned and operated by the Parks Service of the local council. As medium-sized cemeteries go, it is superbly maintained with a small but well-kept Victorian Gothic style cemetery chapel.

The gradient of the crowded hill makes it quite a sight. The paths near the entrance are narrow and give a fairly rural impression, and the place as a whole looks very well-manicured, like a football pitch on a hot August day.

Despite its pristine appearance, memorable monuments are few. However, a bronze harp set in granite, dating from 1929, marks the grave of musician **Anna Sabatini**, and a memorial to five munition workers killed at the local Brocks factory stands close by.

Twickenham Cemetery (1868)

Hospital Bridge Road, Whitton, Middlesex, TW2 6DG
Tel: 020 8876 4511
Transport: Whitton Rail (South-West Trains from Waterloo);
Bus 110, H22, R62
Open: Daily 10am-6.30pm (Apr-Oct), 10am-4.30pm (Nov-Mar)

Situated between Hospital Bridge Road and Percy Road, Twickenham Cemetery presents a fairly flat landscape, but with a well-mown lawn and gleaming marble monuments among a plentiful array of trees. The Decorated-style chapels look suitably eerie with three crow-bearing spires.

The most memorable grave is the bizarre, rock-like monument to **Francis Francis** *(1822-92)*. Both an angler and novelist, he was angling editor of *The Field* for 25 years, and it's possible to make out a line of fishing tackle etched onto his stone. Winchester Cathedral also houses a memorial to him.

Possibly the most recognizable name associated with stamp dealing is **Stanley Gibbons** *(1840-1913)*, who can be found here at Twickenham under his full name Edward Stanley Gibbons. He began stamp dealing in Plymouth with rare stamps acquired from local sailors. He moved to London with his business in 1874 and the rest is philatelic history.

Laurence Oliphant *(1829-1888)* was a contemporary of Sir Richard Burton, the famous explorer, who is buried at St Mary Magdalen's, Mortlake (see page 147). Oliphant travelled widely and reported for *The Times* on the Crimean War. He is best remembered as an early Zionist – arguing for the establishment of a Jewish state in Palestine long before it became a reality.

Notable Residents:

Francis Francis *(1822-96)* – angler and author; **Edward Stanley Gibbons** *(1840-1913)* – stamp dealer; **Laurence Oliphant** *(1829-1888)* – explorer.

THIS IS
CROSSBONE
WWW.CROSS

Oddities

L THE

RAVEYARD

Hell they are tolling the bell for the Whore that lay of The Tabard,
how the carrion crow doth feast in our Crossbones Graveyard
John Constable The Southwark Mysteries

ONES.ORG.UK

The Crossbones Graveyard

Oddities

The Crossbones Graveyard

Union Street, SE1 1SD
www.crossbones.org.uk
Transport: London Bridge or Borough LU;
    Bus 35, 40, 133 (Borough High St / Union St stop)
Open: Wed-Sun 12noon-3pm
    (times vary: please check in advance on 020 7403 3393)

This ancient pauper's graveyard, only a short walk from Borough Market, was unearthed in the 1990s during work on the Jubilee Line extension. The entrance to the site is in Union Street, though many visitors are first attracted by the ribbons and mementos that adorn the old iron gates around the corner in Redcross Way. Even when the graveyard is closed, you can look through these gates into what is now a garden of remembrance.

Crossbones was a pauper's burial ground dating back at least to the 17th century. Local tradition has long identified it as a burial ground for 'poors and whores', including the 'Winchester Geese' who worked in the many licensed brothels of Southwark's Bankside. Despite being licensed by the Bishop of Winchester (whose ruined palace can still be seen close to Southwark Cathedral) these medieval working girls were buried on unconsecrated ground. They were joined by actors and paupers, criminals from the area's many houses of correction and other outsiders deemed too lowly to lie in sacred ground.

The graveyard was closed in 1853, described as being 'completely overcharged with dead', and remained forgotten until uncovered during work on the tube extension when workmen started digging up human remains. The Museum of London estimates that it contains the mortal remains of approximately 15,000 Londoners, more than half of them children.

Many of the aforementioned ribbons on the shrine bear the names and dates of some of those buried at Crossbones – but who places them here? This shrine goes back to 'The Halloween of Crossbones', a ritual drama by local writer John Constable, which was performed every Halloween from 1998 to 2010. The ritual culminated in a procession to the gates of Crossbones, where the names of the dead were read aloud and their ribbons tied to the gates. This event led to the formation of the Friends of Crossbones group.

Since June 2004, at 7pm on the 23rd of every month, the group conducts a Vigil to renew the shrine and to remember the outsiders buried here. Having initially created an unofficial guerrilla garden on the burial ground, Friends of Crossbones worked with Bankside Open Spaces Trust, to establish a public garden of remembrance. Crossbones is part of a larger site owned by Transport for London, who have stated that the garden will be protected from any development of the rest of the site, though its future is still far from certain. Despite these ongoing challenges, Crossbones Graveyard remains a unique landmark, attracting visitors from all over the world, celebrating a bawdy, alternative history of London and its people.

The Pet Cemetery of Hyde Park

Behind Victoria Gate, Bayswater Road, W2 2LU
Transport: Lancaster Gate LU, Bus 46, 94
www.royalparks.org.uk
Open: Currently closed to the public

Set in a quiet corner of the famous park (just off the Bayswater Road) is Victoria Gate Lodge's garden. It is a small and rather hidden area that requires a careful search to find but once located it's not too hard to spot the masses of densely-packed gravestones that surely prove, if proof was needed, that the English are obsessed with their canine 'best friends'.

There are over 300 graves but little 'Cherry', a Maltese Terrier was the first resident. Cherry belonged to the children of Mr. & Mrs. J Lewis Barned, who frequently visited Hyde Park. When Cherry died of old age they approached Mr. Winbridge the lodge-keeper to ask if they could lay Cherry to rest in his back garden, close to the park where they had enjoyed many happy times together. Permission was granted and a tombstone bearing the inscription 'Poor Cherry. Died April 28. 1881' was erected in his memory.

The second dog to be buried was 'Prince' who belonged to the wife of the Duke of Cambridge and who, like many an unfortunate animal in Hyde Park, met his end under the wheels of a carriage! His gravestone simply reads 'Poor Little Prince'.

The inscriptions reveal the emotion these pets drew from their owners and are in stark contrast to the usual notions we have of the austere Victorian era:

Here lie two faithful creatures, Snap and Peter.
'We are only sleeping master.'

Memory of Jim – a little dog with a big heart.

Huguenot Burial Ground

East Hill, Wandsworth, SW18 2QZ

Transport: Clapham Junction or Wandsworth Town Rail;
   Bus 37, 39, 77A, 156, 170, 337

Tel: 020 3959 0060

Near the centre of Wandsworth stands this historic burial ground which was established in 1687 as part of the French Church which stood opposite the parish church of All Saints in Wandsworth.

A walled garden of 30 square metres, it was used by Huguenot refugees fleeing religious persecution in Catholic France who settled in Wandsworth during the 16th and 17th centuries. The burial ground later became known as Mount Nod and twice had to be enlarged, in 1700 and in 1735. It was closed in 1854 and later reopened as a public garden.

At the east end a footpath separates the burial ground from St Mary Magdalen Roman Catholic Church.

The Huguenot refugees differed in social status and the graves here vary considerably from small tablets, which have now become illegible with the passage of time, to large tombs demonstrating considerable wealth. One such historic tomb belongs Peter Paggen (d.1720) of Wandsworth Manor House. The Paggen crest of arms is still visible at both ends of the tomb, as is the name of his daughter, Katherine, who married into the British aristocracy.

In 1911 a stone memorial was erected to the memory of the Wandsworth Huguenots. At one end is a brick wall on which there is a small brass plaque with the following inscription: 'In the nation that is not, nothing stands that stood before, there revenges are forgot, and the hater hates no more.' The plaque was put up in memory of the 300th anniversary of the revocation of the Edict of Nantes, after which many Huguenots were forced to leave France and settle in Britain to avoid Catholic persecution.

The burial ground has undergone numerous restorations over the years. It has been closed since 2011 to allow for the repair of unsafe graves and to improve the paths. There are plans to reopen the space –contact the above number for current access information.

The Paggen family tomb

Necropolis Line
– one way tickets only

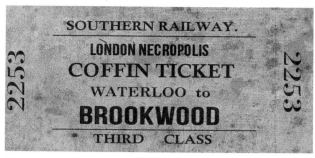

The problems that bedevilled London by virtue of its overcrowded churchyards – poor sanitation, terrible stenches, the cholera epidemics of the 1820s and 30s – drew many suggestions as to how to address the problem besides the familiar one of the garden cemeteries of the 1830s.

By 1850 the idea of one massive metropolitan burial ground that could serve all of London and its burgeoning suburbs was considered by Parliament, and in 1852 the London Necropolis & National Mausoleum Company was granted an Act of Parliament. Two years later the Brookwood Cemetery was opened (see Outer London chapter on page 231), 25 miles outside London with a high speed shuttle ferrying mourners and coffins alike from a specially constructed platform on the eastern side of Waterloo station – a one-way tickets for some.

The dedicated station at Waterloo was first located between York (now Leake) Street and Westminster Bridge Road but was demolished in 1902 due to reconstruction of the entire Waterloo terminus (an appropriate word in this context). The replacement Necropolis Station was built at 121 Westminster Bridge Road.

Initially it was a huge success. Train travel was still quite a novel idea – Stephenson's 'Rocket' was a recent memory – and the burial service offered was affordable and free of the health hazards of the capital. Black-clad steam trains rolled out of the grime of London to the hills of Surrey up to a dozen times a day at Brookwood's peak.

There were doubts though – some were convinced that riding a train to your final destination was not in keeping with the dignity of death. Others were more concerned with class distinction and ensuring that their loved ones remains would be kept apart from those of lesser morals. The Bishop of London argued that: 'For instance, the body of some profligate spendthrift might be placed in a conveyance with the body of some respectable member of the church, which would shock the feelings of his friends.'

To get around these difficulties, the Necropolis Company decided to segregate their cargo. In death as in life there were beautifully decorated first class berths down to third class accommodation that was almost as bad as the Piccadilly Line at rush hour, little more than standing room only. There were also religious distinctions, between Church of England and Nonconformism, which eventually led to separate trains going into separate stations at Brookwood itself. Nonconformists were taken straight to their part of the burial ground in the sunnier north, while Church of England coffins were conveyed to the colder, damper south as the line split into two.

By the 1930s though, the service had slipped to just a couple of trains a week, as suburban cemeteries grew in conjunction with the outward spread of London's commuter population. The Necropolis Station at Waterloo was heavily bombed in April 1941 and was never replaced, though it is still possible to see its entrance at 121 Westminster Bridge Road which still exists as part of the revamped Waterloo Station.

The concept of the Necropolis railway was revived for one last time in 1979 when Waterloo was the departure point for the funeral train that took IRA bomb victim Lord Mountbatten to his final resting place, Romsey Abbey, near the family's home in Hampshire.

The Steamboat of the Dead

Social reformer Edwin Chadwick helped pave the way for the establishment of the first classic Victorian cemeteries but not all his plans came to fruition. After the Necropolis Railway had proved itself to be a roaring success, Chadwick turned his attention to the waterways of the capital.

His plan was the 'Great Eastern Cemetery', to be built at Abbey Wood in what is now part of London, using the Thames as the thoroughfare, almost a hundred 'passengers' a day were to float eastwards from various boarding points using steamboats specially adapted for the purpose.

The cemetery was destined to be a sight worth seeing – avenues full of towering statues, a chapel contained within a gigantic stained-glass dome and a glass covered walkway to ensure that mourners were kept safe from the London weather.

One thing that Chadwick hadn't counted on was the damage his plan would wreak on London's atmosphere. The downfall of Chadwick's grand idea came when medical authorities ruled that odious, noxious gases from the bodies would pollute the river. Parliament had recently suffered the 'Great Stink' and was therefore particularly sensitive to any scheme that might pollute the Thames any further.

The 'Pyramid Cemetery' that wasn't

Today London's skyline is dominated by high-rise landmarks such as Canary Wharf, The Shard and Heron Tower. However, had Thomas Willson's 19th-century idea been accepted, they would all be dwarfed by a pyramid containing millions of dead bodies.

Willson's radical solution to the problem of overcrowded churchyards was in 1829 to propose a pyramid-shaped skyscraper on Primrose Hill that would stand higher than St Paul's Cathedral. With room for five million, it would have been destined for a long shelf-life, and plans stated that it would be 'compact, ornamental and hygienic.' It was to be constructed in brick with polished granite inner walls, with steam-powered lifts and steep internal walkways taking mourners and their dead up 94 floors.

Willson wrote: '...to toil up its singular passages to the summit, will beguile the hours of the curious and impress feelings of solemn awe and admiration upon every beholder'. An obelisk at the top would have sealed its place as London's biggest landmark – had it ever been built. With four entrances on each of its sides, the pyramid would have resembled a building from Ancient Egypt hovering on the edge of Camden Town. It wouldn't have come cheap for its customers either – at an expected price of £50 per vault, making a place there prohibitive to all but the wealthy.

Appendix

Useful Resources

British Library
96 Euston Road, NW1 2DB
Switchboard 0870 444 1500
Reader Admissions 020 7412 7677
A wonderful selection of original manuscripts.

www.londoncemeteries.co.uk
The late and much missed Sue Bailey's incredible, comprehensive
photographic record of the cemeteries of London.

www.findagrave.com
A worldwide database of who lies where, with separate functions
for searching the famous and non-famous. Very much geared
towards burial areas in the USA but with a substantial UK content.

www.derelictlondon.com
Snapshots of the capital's beautiful urban decay: graffiti, buildings,
waterways, cemeteries, murals, pubs, disused tube stations.

www.londongardenstrust.org
The website of this charity has lots of useful information, articles
and pictures relating to London's cemeteries.

www.londonopenhouse.org
London's biggest architectural 'exhibition' gives everyone the
opportunity to visit over 600 buildings new and old across London.

www.cemeteryfriends.com
National Federation of Cemetery Friends.

Appendix

www.fthcp.org
Website run by The Friends of Tower Hamlets Cemetery Park.

www.kensalgreen.co.uk
Kensal Green Cemetery 'Friends' society website.

www.mausolea-monuments.org.uk
The Mausolea and Monuments Trust who restore mausolea around the country.

www.fonc.org.uk
The Nunhead Cemetery 'Friends' society website is a really useful resource which includes details of forthcoming events.

www.fownc.org
West Norwood Cemetery 'Friends' society website with details of future tours and events.

www.highgate-cemetery.org
Highgate Cemetery 'Friends' society website.

www.abneypark.org
Abney Park Cemetery Trust.

www.brompton-cemetery.org.uk
The Friends of Brompton Cemetery.

www.tbcs.org.uk
Brookwood Cemetery Society.

Glossary of Victorian Memorial Symbols

Birds/Animals

Birds in flight – These symbolise the 'winged soul' ascending to heaven. The use of birds to represent the soul goes back as far as ancient Egypt.

Chicken or Rooster - Those that have been woken by the crowing of a cockerel will understand the use of poultry to represent awakening.

Dog – Representing loyalty and the worthiness of the master.

Dove – The dove has long symbolised the Holy Spirit, soul, peace and spirituality. When carrying an olive sprig it represents hope.

Eagle – Representing courage and possibly a military career.

Fish – A long established symbol of faith.

Horse – This represents courage or generosity.

Lamb – A frequently used image on children's graves, symbolizing Christ's sacrifice and the qualities of innocence, gentleness and humility.

Lion – Symbolizes strength generally and specifically the power of God. The lion is thought to guard against evil spirits and represents the beauty of the immortal soul.

Owl – Wisdom.

Swallow – This bird symbolizes a child or motherhood.

Serpent – This symbolized life and health in Ancient Egypt. When depicted swallowing its tail it represents Eternity.

Objects

Anchor – This can indicate the sea-faring occupation of the deceased or more generally represent hope and steadfastness.

Angels – They are an obvious religious symbol. Individual angels can be identified by the objects they carry: Michael bears a sword, Gabriel carries a horn. An angel blowing a trumpet represents the day of judgment. Angels are frequently depicted escorting the deceased to heaven.

Arch or Gate – The victory of life or victory in death.

Arrow – This represents the arrow of time or mortality.

Broken column – Usually represents a life cut short or the loss of the head of the family. It also symbolizes decay and the inevitability of death.

Broken or severed flower – This is a sign of early or sudden death. A severed bud denotes the death of a child.

Candle with a flame – This symbolizes life.

Celtic Cross – The main circle around the crosspiece represents eternity. It originates from the British Celtic cultures.

Cherub's Head – A symbol for the soul.

Circle – Eternity and life everlasting.

Doors and gates – Represent the gates of Heaven and the passage into the afterlife.

Drapery – This indicates sorrow and mourning.

Hands clasped – Representative of marriage or a close bond which lasts even after death. The first to die holds the other's hand, guiding the spouse to heaven. Clasped hands also mean a farewell or last good-bye.

WE SHALL MEET AGAIN

Glossary

Hand pointing upward – A symbol of life after death and ascension to heaven for the righteous.

Hand pointing downward – Represents mortality or sudden death.

Heart – Love, courage and intelligence.

Hourglass – Representing the passage of time and transience of life. On its side means that time has stopped for the deceased.

IHS – An abbreviation of the word for Jesus in Greek, known as the 'sacred monogram'.

Lamp – Representing the light of knowledge and truth.

Moon – Rebirth.

Mourning figure – An early 20th century funerary image.

Obelisk – The obelisk was the Egyptian symbol for the sun god Ra who held the power to recreate. It represents eternal life and health.

Pyramid - It was thought a pyramid-shaped tombstone prevented the devil from reclining on a grave. The pyramid also symbolizes eternity.

Rocks – Representing St Peter and the rock of faith.

Set square and compasses – This is a Masonic symbol but was also used to denote an architect.

Sextant – Used to indicate a navigator or explorer.

Torch – A Greek symbol of life and truth. An inverted torch represents life's extinction.

Urn – A Greek symbol of mourning and the body as a vessel of the soul. Draped it represents death, often of an older person.

Woman clinging to cross, pillar or anchor – This represents faith as does a woman with or without a Bible pointing upward.

Plants

During the 19th century the use of floral symbols became so popular that almost every common flower had a symbolic meaning attached to it.

Daisy – Innocence.

Fleur-de-lis – Flame, passion, ardour and mother.

Forget-me-not – Remembrance.

Hawthorn - Hope, merriness and springtime.

Holly – Foresight.

Honeysuckle – Bonds of love, generosity and devoted affection.

Ivy – Friendship, fidelity, faithfulness, evergreen memories.

Laurel branch, leaves – Represents special achievement, distinction, heroism and the triumph of worldly accomplishment.

Lily – Representing the Virgin Mary, purity and resurrection. Often used on women's graves to represent the restored innocence of the soul in death.

Lily of the valley – Purity and humility.

Oak tree – Representing stability, strength, honour, eternity, endurance. Oak was thought to be the tree from which Jesus Christ's cross was made.

Palm – The triumph of life over death through resurrection.

Pansy – Remembrance and humility.

Passion flower – The passion of Christ. The corona represents the crown of thorns, the three stigmas stand for the three nails, the five anthers the five wounds and the five petals and the five sepals symbolize the ten Apostles.

Poppy – Eternal sleep, rest.

Glossary

Rose – Representing love, beauty, hope and goodness and associated with the Virgin Mary and the 'rose without thorns.' A red rose stands for martyrdom and a white rose means purity.

Thistle – Christ's crown of thorns and earthly sorrow.

Tree – The tree of life. A severed branch represents mortality and a sprouting branch means life everlasting.

Willow tree – A symbol of sorrow and mourning.

Wheat Gathered – Representing the divine harvest and often used for someone dying in later life.

Wreath or Garland - Meaning victory in Death.

Yew tree – Evergreen, life after death.

Bibliography

The following publications have been invaluable sources of information when researching this book:

The Brookwood Necropolis Railway, *John Clarke* (Oakwood Press, 1995) – a history of the train line that took mourners and the deceased to Woking's Brookwood Cemetery from 1854 to 1941.

Permanent Londoners, *Judi Culbertson & Tom Randall* (Robson Books, 1991) – a highly informative step-by-step wander through many of London's cemeteries and churchyards, with chunky biographies of those who really made a difference.

Secret London, *Andrew Duncan* (New Holland, 1998) – a fascinating trawl under the streets of the capital, including special transport networks, secret tunnels, expired rivers and of course burial areas.

The Green London Way, *Bob Gilbert* (Lawrence & Wishart, 1991) – an interesting approach to walking through London's landscapes.

Who Lies Where, *Michael Kerrigan* (Fouth Estate, 1995) – a nationwide look at cemeteries and churchyards that feature well-known names among their residents.

Eccentric London, *Benedict le Vay* (Bradt, 2002) – an off-beat but very informative guide to the parts of London not always mentioned in the usual handbooks. Highly recommended.

London Cemeteries, An Illustrated Guide and Gazetteer, *Hugh Meller* (Ashgate, 1991) – the 'granddaddy' of all books on London's cemeteries. Thoroughly researched and annotated.

Who's Buried Where in London, *Peter Matthews (Shire, 2017)* A detailed account of the most notable names to be found in London's Cemeteries.

Index

Index

Index

Index

Index

Index

About us:

Metro is a small independent publishing company with a
reputation for producing well-researched and beautifully-
designed guides on many aspects of London life.
In fields of interest as diverse as shopping, bargain hunting,
architecture, the arts, and food, our guide books contain special
tips you won't find anywhere else.

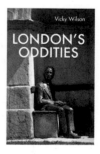

www.metropublications.com

London's Hidden Walks Series

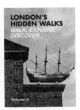

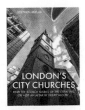

CAROLIN
DARLING WI
AND GRA
1910

Highgate Cemetery